"Orlando Crespo writes with clarity and sensitivity. In *Being Latino in Christ,* he addresses the daunting task of defining what it means to be a second-generation Latino in the United States. More important, he defines what it means to be Latinos who have chosen the road less traveled of following Christ, embracing and even celebrating the heritage and culture we have been blessed with by our Creator. The book serves as a guide for those of us who desire to integrate all of who we are with our faith in Christ."

RUDY HERNANDEZ
Board of Trustees, InterVarsity
Christian Fellowship/USA

"*Being Latino in Christ* is an exceptional work because it provides emotional and spiritual holism to second-generation Latinos who struggle with identity. There are also many helps for other second-generation ethnic groups."

DR. MANUEL ORTIZ
Professor of Mission and Urban Ministry Emeritus
Westminster Theological Seminary

CONTENTS

To *mi familia* Crespo.
To my loving wife, Maritza, who has always affirmed me in ministry and still "likes me."
To my son Daniel who taught me to be honest even when it hurt.
To my son David who taught me to be myself no matter who might be watching.
To my parents, Francisco and Casilda, for loving me unconditionally.
To my brother, Edwin, and sisters Marilyn, Sandra and Milagro
for always being there when I needed them most.

InterVarsity Press
P.O. Box 1400, Downers Grove, IL 60515-1426
World Wide Web: www.ivpress.com
E-mail: mail@ivpress.com

InterVarsity Press® *is the book-publishing division of InterVarsity Christian Fellowship/USA*®*, a student movement active on campus at hundreds of universities, colleges and schools of nursing in the United States of America, and a member movement of the International Fellowship of Evangelical Students. For information about local and regional activities, write Public Relations Dept., InterVarsity Christian Fellowship/USA, 6400 Schroeder Rd., P.O. Box 7895, Madison, WI 53707-7895, or visit the IVCF website at <www.ivcf.org>.*

Design: Cindy Kiple
Images: Schalkwijk/Art Resource, NY
ISBN 0-8308-2374-3

Printed in the United States of America ∞

Library of Congress Cataloging-in-Publication Data

Crespo, Orlando, 1963-
  Being Latino in Christ: finding wholeness in your ethnic identity/
Orlando Crespo.
    p. cm.
Includes bibliographical references.
  ISBN 0-8308-2374-3 (pbk.: alk. paper)
  1. Hispanic Americans—Religion. 2. Ethnicity—Religious
aspects—Christianity. I. Title.
  BR563.H57C74 2003
  277.3'0089'68—dc22

                                                          2003016146

P	17	16	15	14	13	12	11	10	9	8	7	6	5	4	3	2	1
Y	15	14	13	12	11	10	09	08	07	06	05	04	03				

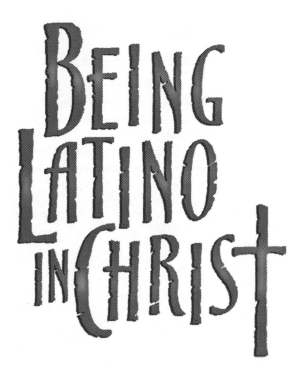

BEING LATINO IN CHRIST

Finding Wholeness
in Your Ethnic Identity

ORLANDO CRESPO

IVP

InterVarsity Press
Downers Grove, Illinois

INTRODUCTION

Hispanic Americans have been here for so long, and yet kept their identity, that it is rather doubtful they will follow the same process of assimilation by which Swedes, Irish and Italians joined mainstream American society. Especially now that there is an increasing awareness of the value of one's culture and traditions, it seems safe to predict that Hispanic Americans will be around mañana (tomorrow), and for as many mañanas as it pleases God to grant to this country. . . . Hispanic Americans . . . are going back to their historic roots and affirming their distinctive, not as something of which to be ashamed or to hide from view but as something of which to be proud and to exhibit at every possible opportunity.

JUSTO GONZÁLEZ, *MAÑANA: CHRISTIAN THEOLOGY FROM A HISPANIC PERSPECTIVE*

In 1999 I saw a movie, *Bicentennial Man* starring Robin Williams, that struck a chord in me as a Latino in the United States. In the movie robots have become enormously sophisticated; their design includes human along with mechanical anatomy, intermingling and interconnecting. If either human or mechanical elements malfunctioned, the robot would stop working. In the climax of the movie a human robot, played by Williams, goes before a world congress, which debates the dignity and worth of these new hybrid beings and whether they deserve to have the same rights as fully human beings. The film's most intriguing and under-developed aspect involves the portrayal of a society of humans who re-sist full acceptance of the humanized robots.

The U.S. Latino experience is like this. Those of us who have been born and raised in this country are a new breed of Latinos/Americans in whom both identities are in operation and who struggle for acceptance in both parent cultures. We are not one or the other. We are both. In *Living in Spanglish: The Search for Latino Identity in America,* Ed Morales puts it this way: "Latino culture, particularly our Spanglish American varia-tion, has never been about choosing affiliation with a particular race—it is a space where multiple levels of identification are possible. . . . If the postmodern era is characterized by unprecedented heterogeneity and randomness, then Latinos are well prepared to take advantage of it."[1]

I have spent much of my life in this space of multiple identifications, fighting not to choose one over the other, but living in the blessings and contradictions of both. I have decided that I love being somewhere in the middle of both my Latino and American worlds. It has been a place of sadness as I have had to face the cultural weaknesses of each, but some-how instead of becoming bitter, I have been filled with God's comfort and strength as he has come close to me. I have come to realize that my Latino identity in this country—a conjoining of two ethnic identities—is about God designing a new breed he is pleased to use to influence both cultures and the world.

As a follower of Christ, I have chosen a new path of trust. This trust is no longer based on my own instinct, which is frequently distorted with my own fears, but on the reality that God is committed to my well-being. I have chosen courage because it is the thing I lack most. If I can be coura-

---

[1]Ed Morales, *Living in Spanglish: The Search for Latino Identity in America* (New York: St. Martin's Press, 2002), p. 17.

geous—and this is where the cutting edge of my faith rests—then my obedience to Christ truly has meaning and his power can be manifest in and through me. I have reasons to pity myself, but my faith in Christ has blocked the natural course of my self-loathing. I know too much about God to sit back and do nothing. I have therefore chosen to walk into the confusion of biculturalism, trusting that God will be in those places waiting for me. The Apostle Paul said it well when he faced his weaknesses and said: "Three times I pleaded with the Lord to take it away from me. But he said to me, 'My grace is sufficient for you, for my power is made perfect in weakness.' Therefore I will boast all the more gladly about my weaknesses, so that Christ's power may rest on me. That is why, for Christ's sake, I delight in weaknesses, in insults, in hardships, in persecutions, in difficulties. For when I am weak, then I am strong" (2 Corinthians 12:8-10).

This is why I have chosen to think and write about my experience of growing as a Latino Christian, a journey of knowing more about the multidimensionality God has created in me. Understanding myself in the realm of ethnicity has informed me about the goodness and power of God. And knowing the love of God has led me to embrace who I am as a Latino. I want to share my sorrows and joys with you, hoping that my journey of self-understanding may help you snap together some pieces of the puzzle of your own life.

As a second-generation Latino, I write this book for other second- (and third- and fourth-) generation Latinos who are trying to hold in tension their dual identity. While the media is giving increased recognition to Latino culture in the United States, many young Latinos still do not know how to incorporate their ethnic identity into who they are as people. They often swing to extremes, from totally assimilating into American mainstream culture to believing that the Latino culture is superior to all others.

In this book I argue that most Latinos born in the United States will be happiest somewhere in between. I seek to point us toward a healthy balance as we gain a conceptual understanding of Latino ethnic identity and learn how to practically live out our God-given strengths and gifts.

Here is a brief synopsis of what you can expect. Chapter one tells of my own journey toward ethnic self-discovery. In chapter two I explore a new Latino identity that has less to do with the country of origin— although it starts there—and more to do with the Latino experience in the United States. My goal in this chapter is also to broaden the net of who is "Latino" when many are questioning if they are Latino enough. Please note that for the sake of brevity I am using the term *Latino* in a way that encompasses Latino males and Latina females in the United States.

Chapter three includes a grid to help you map out where you stand in your own journey of assimilation and identification. Since it is important to understand the roots of the sense of inferiority that continues to plague large portions of the Latino community, chapter four takes a look at the phenomenon of *mestizaje,* the mixing of races. In chapter five I turn to Scripture to meet biblical characters like Moses, Esther, Mordecai, Jesus and Paul who lived out of their ethnicity and allowed God to use it as a catalyst to accomplish his plans in their lives and his purposes in the world. Chapter six defines culture and describes how our ethnicity and our faith can work hand in hand to shape us into healthy, whole people, able to honor God and love our neighbors.

Chapters seven, eight and nine address very practical issues about how we need to move beyond ourselves. A strong bicultural Latino identity is not just about coming to terms with who we are but also about positioning ourselves to serve others through racial reconciliation. We can no longer remain on the margins of discussions about race, hesitant to contribute our views for fear of rejection or inadequacy. We must believe God has something to say to others through our gifts as a community.

Chapter nine offers ideas for how you can give back and facilitate growth in others who need to grow in their ethnic identity. Years ago a Latina professor, the only one at Colgate University at the time, ingrained in my head and heart that I was not in college just to advance myself; I was there to give back *y para enriquecer la comunidad Latina* (to enrich the Latino community). This entire book, in fact, is my way of giving something back to my Latino community, a community I love and respect and am proud to be a part of.

Finally, in chapter ten I call on Latinos to step into positions of leadership to contribute to making our communities, our churches and our nation stronger and healthier. I also issue a warning not to make ethnic identity an idol. We must invite God into our ethnic journey so that we give it the appropriate level of attention. In doing so we become healthy and whole people who embrace all we are without falling into idolatry of ethnicity and culture.

I have spent the last sixteen years serving in campus ministry with InterVarsity Christian Fellowship. Many of the stories I tell and examples I use come from that context. InterVarsity as a movement has worked very hard at issues of ethnic diversity. Our growth in this area has come from great successes but also difficult failures and painful problems that have felt insurmountable. Multiethnicity is, in fact, complex and messy. Nevertheless, most of what I have learned about Latino ethnic identity has come from dialogue and interaction with fellow campus ministers who are part of LaFe (Latino Fellowship), InterVarsity's Latino ministry. I am indebted to them for entering into this journey with me, a journey that has elevated and enriched all of us with tears, deep emotions and growth toward wholeness.

Finally, I realize that my experience may be very different from yours, but perhaps there is enough that will ring true and give you greater insight into your experience. This is my journey, and I am inviting you to look into it and see what you can find to help in your own ethnic journey.

I have never hidden my mistakes from my two sons because I want them to be better men than I am myself. As you read this book I hope you will read the lines and between the lines. And after you have read, I hope the Holy Spirit, who is our Counselor, will take my simple words and make you a person who can love and receive love, a person who is not afraid of life. A person who can dream big. A person who hears God and can live to please him. By all means learn from my mistakes, my struggles and my insights. May this book help you find wholeness in your ethnic identity, lead you to glorify God and fill you with compassion for others in need.

1

❀

MY JOURNEY TOWARD A
LATINO ETHNIC IDENTITY

My frame was not hidden from you
when I was made in the secret place.
When I was woven together in the depths of the earth,
your eyes saw my unformed body.

PSALM 139:15-16

W hen I was seven years old my parents decided to move our family into
a predominantly White neighborhood of Italian, Irish and Polish immigrants in Springfield, Massachusetts. Bursting with excitement and energy during the first week in our new home, we spent much of our time
in our new backyard, vigorously raking up crabapples that had fallen
from our apple tree. The lawn had not been raked for years, and the more
we raked, the more layers of crabapples we uncovered. But it didn't matter: this was our new home, an opportunity to reach for our dreams, a
place where my four siblings and I could live in safety with a backyard to
play in. It was truly an exciting season of our lives, and we couldn't wait
to get everything in order, even those mushy, smelly crabapples.

As we raked and filled bag after bag with apples, neighbors passed by, peering into our backyard to see who their new neighbors were. They saw that we looked Latino, and no one approached us to welcome us. A neighbor across the street was outright angry when he discovered we were "Spics" (a derogatory name used for Hispanics in the 1970s). He revealed his disgust every time we played stickball on the street and the ball accidentally rolled onto his property. With resentment and hatred in his eyes he would glare at us and order us to get out of his yard and his neighborhood. "You don't belong here. Go back to Puerto Rico where you belong!" he'd say, unaware that we had been born and raised in Springfield and had never even visited Puerto Rico.

At such moments I felt confused. I couldn't understand why he was so disgusted with us. What was so bad about a ball going into his front yard? I made a mental note to stay out of this man's way. I was afraid that next time he might try to hurt me.

This neighbor watched us like a hawk, taking note of every little thing we did. It became so extreme and frustrating for my family that we nicknamed him Nosy Charlie, which conveniently described both his attitude and his large protruding nose. Only decades later did I fully comprehend the concept of racism and the impact of bigotry in my life, beginning in those first weeks of moving into our new home. Not long after my family moved in, the neighbor and his family moved out.

A 1972 article in *New York* magazine captured the sentiments of millions of Whites who were similarly being forced to interact with Puerto Ricans moving into their neighborhoods.

These people were "Spanish." They came in swarms like ants turning the sidewalks brown, and they settled in, multiplied, whole sections of the city fallen to their shiny black raincoats and chewing-gum speech. We called them "meedahs," [from the word *mira*, meaning "look" or "look over here"] because they were always shouting "mee-dah, mee-dah." . . . I only knew they grew in numbers rather than stature, that they were neither white nor black but some indelicate tan, and that they were here, irrevocably; the best you could do to avoid contamination was to keep them out of mind.[1]

To survive such hatred of Puerto Ricans, I learned to live in two worlds even as an adolescent. At home I spoke Spanish, ate Puerto Rican food, danced salsa and merengue with my three sisters, and enjoyed cultural events like Parrandas—fiestas during the Christmas season—with my extended family. But when I walked out the front door and joined my White friends in the neighborhood, I left behind my Puerto Rican identity and tried to assimilate as thoroughly as possible. In fact, because of my light complexion some of my new friends in junior high school did not notice that I was Puerto Rican. I enjoyed letting them assume I was White, because they treated me as one of their own.

The moment they discovered I was Puerto Rican, the look on their faces and their attitudes changed. "You're Puerto Rican? I can't believe it. I thought you were White." In other words, *I thought you were OK. Now I don't know anymore.* They were not mean to me, but something felt different. They seemed more aloof and less interested in me. They didn't seek me out the way they used to. As a young teenager very attuned to my emotions, I could feel the difference and I hated it. But instead of brushing this off and seeing their ignorance, I internalized my feelings and saw myself as "less than."

On the way home after one of these incidents I imagined what it

---

[1]Richard Goldstein, "The Big Mango," *New York*, August 7, 1972.

would be like to be White all the time and not just at certain times. *I'll never tell anyone I'm Puerto Rican unless they figure it out on their own,* I thought. *That way I can feel like one of them and fit in all the time.* Somehow I knew this idea would never work and would only lead to greater pain in the end.

I was not proud to be Puerto Rican. We were told we were dirty, loud, uneducated, immoral and unable to speak English "good." These were the stereotypes I internalized and learned to live with every day as I stepped out into the White world. But at home I received a different message. Our mother, Casilda, loved us and valued education highly. She taught us to study hard. Our father, Francisco, worked himself to the bone to allow us a better life. Our grandparents, Ramón and Alejandra, had a marriage that had endured despite social pressure on their family. My older brother, Edwin, took me wherever he went and was my protector. My sisters, Marilyn, Sandra and Milagro, affirmed me in all I did and believed in me when I could not. In all it was the love of *mi familia,* their warmth, nurture and sacrifices, that initially sheltered me from the hard blows of prejudice, racism and alienation.

I wish I could write that the alienation I felt from prejudice didn't hurt me, but it did. It left its ugly imprint on my soul. It seems that some Latinos have been able to let hurtful events roll off their backs like water. I admire and commend them, but I am not one of them.

Given my struggles, I am surprised at how successful I have been and how much I have accomplished. I have received numerous athletic, drama and ministry awards. How can someone overcome by low self-worth succeed in so much? It is because God has revealed his love for all that I am—including my Latino identity at crucial moments in my life.

In times of reflection, as I have allowed my pain to surface, God has kept bringing me back to the truth that he made me with great intentionality and purpose. When I wanted to abandon my identity as a Latino, God picked up all the pieces I wanted to leave behind.

My faith in Jesus Christ and my identity are inextricably bound up together. I am not only a Christian: I am a Christian who is Latino, and I am a Latino who is a Christian.

In this chapter I invite you to take a journey with me as I revisit the events, relationships and circumstances that God used to build my ethnic identity. Like any long journey, mine is filled with rocky terrain of pain and setbacks but also smooth terrain of joy and long strides forward. As if with bright yellow paint used to mark a trail in a wooded area, I will mark the experiences that contributed most to my Latino identity and have moved me toward what theologian Orlando Costas calls a cultural conversion, an awakening to one's ethnic self. Here are the yellow markers for the trail I have discovered on my journey.

1. connecting with others like me

2. embracing the pain of my people

3. understanding Latino complexity and alienation

4. receiving encouragement for the journey

My hope is that these "yellow markers" will help direct your path and make your journey toward wholeness that much easier.

MY TRIP TO PUERTO RICO: CONNECTING WITH OTHERS LIKE ME

When I was thirteen years old, my mother decided it was time for my sisters and me to spend a summer with *Tio Diego, Tia Juanita y nuestra familia en Puerto Rico*. My sisters arrived in Puerto Rico a week earlier than I did. I had to fly alone, having decided to stay to play one more week of Little League baseball.

I was extremely nervous when I got on the plane. I had no idea what to expect and began to feel as if I'd made a terrible mistake. I even thought about asking the flight attendant if I could just stay on the plane and fly back with the crew.

But from the moment I stepped off the plane, something began to stir deep inside of me. Puerto Rico was beautiful. The air was warm and the sun shone brightly. The people were friendly, and they all looked like my family. They spoke Spanish, the language of my parents, the language I resented and thought was stupid. Here Spanish was the norm and Puerto Ricans were the majority. I met family members who were lawyers and studying to be doctors. For the first time in my life I saw well-dressed Puerto Rican businessmen and politicians. *So this is the island my parents talked about with such nostalgia,* I marveled. A lot of things began to make sense as I saw the close resemblance of my parents' cultural ways to the habits of Puerto Ricans I met. Cousins, aunts and uncles I had only heard about loved me without knowing me and welcomed me with kindness, affection and hospitality like I had never experienced before. One of my aunts took me to the very shack where my mother and her family lived. My mom had told me about this place and the hardships they had faced. I felt I got to know my mom a little better and loved her a lot more. This was the summer that I fell in love with my people, my culture, my parents and my land—Puerto Rico, *la Isla del Encanto* (the Island of Enchantment).

This was also the summer I began to love myself and my ethnic identity. I had discovered I belonged to a land and a people who were gracious, intelligent and hospitable. I began to embrace who I was and realize to whom I belonged.

Discovering the beauty of my people and culture was a vital first step in my cultural conversion. It was a decisive moment that God used to offset the overpowering experience of being part of a minority that was looked down on by White America. Through it God began to shape me into a healthy human being and a Christian no longer in denial of his culture and ethnicity.

In Puerto Rico I discovered the value of interacting with others who are like you, who simply by being themselves unfold something in you. What you thought was a personal quirk in yourself or your parents reveals itself as a cultural quality. There is no better way to grow in your ethnic identity than through interactions with others who share your ethnicity.

In recent years when I have led conferences on ethnic identity in various parts of the United States, Latinos arrive reluctant to embrace their identity. By the end of the conference, having interacted with other Latinos, they begin to cherish these new friendships and their shared values and experiences. They discover something about themselves they had no idea was missing. I have seen them weep uncontrollably because they do not want to leave each other. Now that they have found the missing piece, they no longer want to live without it. For many, such connections and the feelings of *familia* mark the beginning of their journey, just as my journey began the moment I stepped off the plane in Puerto Rico.

LATINO HISTORY: EMBRACING THE PAIN OF MY PEOPLE

Understanding the history of racism against Latinos in the United States is another important factor that has helped me embrace my heritage. Learning of such oppression against my people has made me intensely angry and bitter at times. But it has filled me with compassion and love for my people and for others who have suffered injustices.

Several years ago PBS aired a documentary about Puerto Rico called *Mis Dos Casas (My Two Homes)*. It reviewed some of the struggle for an

independent Puerto Rico and the injustices inflicted by the U.S. government. The Ponce Massacre of 1937 was particularly disturbing. As
Puerto Ricans marched peacefully in protest against the arrest and impris-
onment of Pedro Albizo Campos, leader of the Puerto Rican Nationalist
Party, 150 policemen armed with rifles, machineguns, hand grenades
and tear gas bombs opened fire on the unarmed crowd of men, women
and children. When the shooting stopped, 20 people were dead and 150
were wounded. As the women who were not shot helped the dying and
bleeding, their white dresses turned a crimson red. After watching the
program I wept in pain for an hour, as if I had just been told that a family
member had been killed in a terrible accident.

In the 1930s U.S. laboratories and chemical companies used Puerto
Rican women as guinea pigs to test birth control pills. Once the pill was
judged safe for use in the United States, it was no longer available on the
island; there sterilization became the chief method to prevent births. The
U.S. government developed a sterilization campaign to limit the number
of births of Puerto Ricans. Researchers years later report, "Common-
wealth officials told [Puerto Rican women] that their welfare payments
would be cut off unless they agreed to sterilization. Others were told that
they had cancer, and that sterilization would save their lives. With still
other women, the operation was performed in hospitals immediately after delivery. The mother, exhausted by hours of labor, would submit to
the doctor's cold 'logic.'" By 1976 35 percent of Puerto Rican women and
20 percent of the men had undergone sterilization—the highest rate of
sterilization in the world.[2]

I still have much to learn about Puerto Rican history. But the more I
learn, the more I want to become an advocate for change. Puerto Rico's

---

[2]Jane Norling, *Puerto Rico: Flame of Resistance* (San Francisco: Peoples Press, 1977), p. 116.

history is my history because I have chosen to identify fully with the Puerto Rican experience. To do so means I must embrace all of the sadness and the pain of our history. It also means I am willing to speak out against the injustices that have been perpetrated against my people. It is not enough to feel the pain; I must recognize that God is committed to bringing justice. The psalmist in the Old Testament understood God as the Deliverer who conspired against oppressors by ruining their schemes and meeting the needs of those who called on him in a time of need: "I know that the Lord secures justice for the poor and upholds the cause of the needy" (Psalm 140:12).

LATINO IDENTITY:
UNDERSTANDING ITS COMPLEXITY AND ALIENATION

I am also learning to accept the complexity and alienation of being Latino in America. I have accepted that I belong to a new and complex breed that God has put together. I am not just Latino, I am also American. I love and appreciate both cultures. Yet I do not feel completely at home in either one.

When I visit Puerto Rico I am called a *Nuyorican,* a name Puerto Ricans on the island call those of us who grew up in New York City or anywhere other than Puerto Rico. In fact when people found out I was not from New York City but from Massachusetts, they modified this term to fit me better: I was a *Massarican.* While islanders welcome us as family, they do not recognize the dual nature of our identity. The way they see it, if you were not born in Puerto Rico, you are not really Puerto Rican, you are American.

I must constantly function in two worlds, both of which reject me at some level and to neither of which I truly belong. White Americans often see me not as a fellow citizen but as someone of Hispanic descent. Puerto

21

Ricans have been American citizens for over sixty years, yet I am often asked if I am a citizen. When I ride my bike through a White neighborhood I am looked at with suspicion. Ruben Martinez puts it this way in his book about the new Los Angeles: "As for myself it is all too often that I yearn for the other even when I am with the other; nowhere do I feel complete."[3]

Father Virgilio P. Elizondo, founder of the Mexican American Cultural Center in San Antonio and currently rector of the Cathedral of San Fernando in that city, uses the term *mestizaje* (the mixing of people of Spanish and Indian descent) to summarize the struggles of identity many Latinos face in the United States.

> The cultural parent groups of the mestizo normally tend to reject their cultural child and its cultural identity because it does not appear to be the perfect mirror of their own identity. The mestizo is partly their own, but it is partly other and foreign. As a mestizo you are allowed to live, but you are not allowed to have a life of your own. You will always appear deficient by the norms of both parent groups and therefore never fully acceptable to either. Yet the parent cultures are not destroyed in the mestizo, but mutually combined so as to form a new identity.
>
> The great tragedy of mestizo existence is that the parent cultures do not see their child in a loving way, but rather tend to look upon it as a mixture of "good and bad," a misfit, a nonequal. If cultural-spiritual poverty is the worst type of oppression, mestizaje is the worst type of human rejection because it brings with it a double alienation and margination.[4]

---

[3]Ruben Martinez, *The Other Side* (New York: Vintage Books, 1993).
[4]Virgilio P. Elizondo, *Galilean Journey: The Mexican American Promise* (Maryknoll, N.Y.: Orbis, 1983), pp. 98-99.

Living in alienation and marginalization, between two worlds, is often very difficult and lonely. However, the Scriptures have been a source of strength and encouragement in my journey of understanding and embracing myself and my people. Moses' story in particular inspires me. While Moses was not a *mestizo* (someone who is biracial), he did struggle with issues of identity similar to those Latinos face. He was born a Hebrew, was raised as an Egyptian and became a Midianite. And it was this man of three cultures that God called out to confront the pharaoh and free the Hebrew people from slavery:

> "So now, go. I am sending you to Pharaoh to bring my people the Israelites out of Egypt."
>
> But Moses said to God, "Who am I, that I should go to Pharaoh and bring the Israelites out of Egypt?"
>
> And God said, "I will be with you. And this will be the sign to you that it is I who have sent you: When you have brought the people out of Egypt, you will worship God on this mountain." (Exodus 3:10-12)

Moses is asking about his identity when he asks God: "Who am I?" In effect he is saying, "Are you sending me back to the pharaoh as an Egyptian prince, as a Jewish slave or as a Midianite shepherd?" This would have enormous implications for the words he would use and the approach he would take in confronting the pharaoh. It is an honest and important question. What is intriguing to me is that God never gives him an answer. He simply tells Moses to go and that his presence will be with Moses.

God is affirming Moses' triculturalism: "I have created you the way you are, Moses. You are the person I need for this task right now. Go and I will give you all that you need to accomplish what I have set before you."

God uses us where we are, in all our complexity and confusion, especially in our ethnic identity, and does great and wonderful things through us. I have begun to view being Latino and American as a gift and an opportunity God has opened up for me to minister to very different groups of people, to draw them to Christ and toward reconciliation with each other.

Embracing my ethnic identity in all its complexity has become an opportunity to witness to God's greatness. As Moses' confidence came from God, so our trust must be in him to do great things through us even in the midst of our confusion and doubts about who we are. If God embraces us in our complexity and is able to accomplish his purposes through us, how much more should we accept ourselves culturally and ethnically?

RECEIVING ENCOURAGEMENT FOR THE JOURNEY

Another vital element in my journey toward wholeness has been help from others who have embarked on their own ethnic journey. When I first started ministry, I had no idea how much I would grow in my ethnic identity. In campus ministry I discovered it was difficult to avoid coming to terms with who I was as a Latino. I am grateful that many of my colleagues and supervisors encouraged me to explore my roots as a Latino. Frequently I would be asked to speak about the Latino experience in front of students and other campus ministers. These were important moments for me to understand and embrace my identity.

One time my supervisor asked me to give an address about my Latino experience to a group of InterVarsity campus ministers. I was extremely reluctant to do so, sobered by the fact that when I had first started working with Latino students, I failed to capitalize on the momentum several volunteers and others had worked so hard to build.

Our Latino student ministry in New York City, LaFe, had collapsed after I took charge. Still, my supervisor's persistence and the encouragement of others gave me the courage not only to share my Latino experience with others but also to surrender to God the heartache attached to my early failure.

At a more recent InterVarsity Multiethnic Staff Conference—where ethnic-specific departments gather to deal with multiethnicity within our movement—a new campus staffworker, Layla Hanash, experienced the affirmation she desperately needed in her ethnic journey. As a biracial person she struggled with fitting in at the conference. But here is how she summed up the experience in the end:

> I want to tell you how much it meant to me that you included Middle Easterners in the prayer time on the last day. It was funny though, because on the last day of the conference when Alec Hill (president of InterVarsity) introduced the different people groups we'd be praying for and said "Middle Eastern people," I thought, *Whoa, you mean there are other Middle Easterners and I didn't meet them? I have got to meet them!* So the time came, and I waited to see who it was. Then I realized it was me!
>
> I felt so many things in one second, standing alone. I felt a little scared, and even alone. I also felt excited, because I had been hearing that week about how the LaFe group had been pretty much just Orlando Crespo and a few others for a while, and now they are growing. God is growing them! I wanted that for Middle Easterners too! That prayer time was so helpful for me also because it was the first time that I really felt affirmed for being Middle Eastern in InterVarsity. Not just acknowledged, but affirmed in it. It was a great time for me.

It has been a difficult journey, and I have come a long way in understanding and embracing my Latino identity. I have learned much about myself, about God's affirmation of me and about my rich Puerto Rican heritage. I have learned to live above the victimization and accomplish great things in God's strength and grace. He is a God who is for me and travels with me.

Sometimes, though, I wish there were a way to go back to that little Puerto Rican boy raking crabapples and playing stickball, that seven-year-old boy who was me. I would take him by the hand and walk him through his new neighborhood. I would tell him, "Don't be afraid. You're going to be OK. One day you will know who you are and to whom you belong."

QUESTIONS FOR REFLECTION AND DISCUSSION

1. What are the stereotypes, prejudices or bigotry you and your family have had to endure? What effect has this had on you?

2. In what ways have you denied or turned away from your culture and ethnicity?

3. What experiences have made you open to further exploring your ethnic identity?

4. What has been particularly confusing for you as you try to understand yourself ethnically?

5. How has God affirmed you in your ethnic identity?

6. What are some ways you hope to grow in your ethnic identity as you read this book?

2

❀

OUR IDENTITY
AS AMERICAN LATINOS

Here lies Juan
Here lies Miguel
Here lies Milagros
Here lies Manuel
Who died yesterday today
And will die again tomorrow
Always broke
Always owing
Never knowing
That they are a beautiful people
Never knowing the geography of their complexion
PUERTO RICO IS A BEAUTIFUL PLACE
PUERTORRIQUENOS ARE A BEAUTIFUL RACE

PEDRO PIETRI, "THE PUERTO RICAN OBITUARY"

Latinos are the fastest growing minority group in the United States. In 2003 the big news was that Latinos had surpassed Blacks as the nation's largest minority group. Between April 2000 and July 2001 the U.S. Census Bureau estimated that the Latino population had grown from 35.3 million to 37 million—13 percent of the population. As advertisers have tried to figure out effective marketing strategies to implement with this growing population, they are discovering what we as Latinos have always known—we are diverse and similar at the same time. We are from different countries but we speak the same language. We are from different faiths but have the same Catholic roots. Our histories are different, but we have all experienced conquest, colonization and *mestizaje*. We label ourselves differently as well. Some of us prefer to call ourselves Hispanic, Chicano or Latino. Others of us prefer to use terms based on our native countries, such as Argentinian, Ecuadorian or Guatamalen. Still, when we are in a majority setting and discover another Latino in our midst, our differences are put aside and our commonalities rise to the surface with pride as we approach each other as *familia*.

CHOOSING TO IDENTIFY

As we continue to grow in number and diversity, one of the great challenges we face is how to define what it means to be Latino in America. Rudy Hernandez, a San Antonio businessman, gave a lecture at a Latino conference several years ago that had a deep impact on many who were struggling with questions of self-definition. Here I outline some of his thoughts that were most helpful.

Rudy began by outlining several false measures others have used to define Latino identity.

1. *Proximity.* Some define you as Latino if you live in close proximity to a Latin country such as Mexico and behave like the influx of immigrants who have brought their traditions and culture intact.

2. *Language.* Others define you as Latino on the basis of language. If

you speak Spanish, then you are truly Latino. If you don't speak the language, there is no possible way you could be Latino. First-generation Latinos who have retained their language and culture may use this argument and be thoroughly convinced you are not Latino.

3. *Physical features.* Still others use physical features to determine if you are Latino. Of course, the obvious difficulty with this argument is that there is no Latino look. We are as multiracial as a people can get. For example, one of my great-great-grandmothers was Black, the daughter of a Black slave in Puerto Rico. Yet I am light skinned with deep-set eyes. Many Latinos I meet assume I am from the Middle East. My wife, Maritza, who is Afro-Cuban, is partly Chinese: her great-great-grandfather came to Cuba in search of work and to eventually make his way into the United States via Cuba.

4. *Cultural habits.* Another definition is based on cultural habits, such as the music you listen to, the food you eat or do not eat and the traditions you hold. One day a friend of Rudy's told someone else that Rudy was not Hispanic. "He sold out; he may eat a few tacos now and then, but he is not Hispanic anymore." This dismissive statement was very hurtful to Rudy, but it was an incident God used to help him begin to understand what it really meant to be Latino in the United States.

5. *Geographic parameters.* Others will use socioeconomic or geographic parameters to define you. Their picture of a Latino is someone who is poor and lives in "el barrio" or in the Southwest part of the country.

6. *Religious parameters.* Still others use religious parameters to define you, concluding that all Latinos are Catholic. While the majority of Latinos do have Catholicism as part of their background, some Latinos are able to trace their Protestant roots back three or four generations. Also, there are Latinos who are not Catholic or Protestant but practice other religious beliefs.

While all these definitions reflect something of Latino experience, they all fall short of how we should define ourselves as Latinos in the United States. Rudy believes it is a combination of two elements that helps us define who we are. First, somewhere in our family there is a Latino heritage that resonates with us when we are with others of Hispanic heritage. We can trace our heritage back to a Hispanic country. The second important factor is that we willingly *choose to identify* with that heritage by being open about our ethnic roots, taking initiative to learn more about our Latino culture and caring about the issues relevant to our people. These two factors must be present. If you have the heritage piece but have made a conscious choice not to embrace and identify with being Latino, then a strong case could be made that culturally you are not Latino. If on the other hand you strongly identify with Latino culture but do not have the family heritage, you might be considered an honorary Latino but not one by blood. Andrew Gackenbach

One of the most painful experiences for Latinos is when others who see themselves as "truly Latino" reject them based on one of the definitions mentioned above. Jen Huerta Ball, a staff leader for InterVarsity in Los Angeles, has had several painful experiences when *puro* (pure) Latinos decided she was not truly Latina because of how she acted and because she did not speak Spanish. What is ironic is that these same folks would not be considered Latinos themselves by some first-generation Latinos who believe that you are not truly of *la raza* unless you are born in a Latino country. "Every Latino born in America is not Latino but American. To be truly Latino you must have been born in a Latino country." This is how many define being Latino.

It is sad that we Latinos can be so embracing of others and so exclusive in our judgments of each other, adding to the hurt that many second-, third- and fourth-generation Latinos experience growing up as minorities in the United States. Instead of affirming our young people, we tear them down simply because they did not learn to speak Spanish. They are pushed aside as if they have less value by some who see themselves as authentic Latinos but lack the insight to recognize the particular challenges that second- and third-generation Latinos experience day to day.

AMERICAN (U.S.) LATINOS

When the 2000 census was taken, the talk throughout the nation centered on the immense growth of the Latino population, which had surpassed all projections. One surprise, however, that perplexed even Latinos was the fact that the second-largest group of Latinos in the census were those who did not identify a national origin at all. A September 2001 article by Achy Obejas of the *Chicago Tribune* states that while the census form may have been partially at fault for not being specific enough, the decisions not to identify a national origin may point to a new trend in the way Latinos in the United States identify themselves:

> Some observers believe that group—more than 6 million of the nation's 35 millions Latinos—may be the first significant sign of a new and different kind of identity, that of the American Latino. Instead of relying on national origin, language, cuisine or religion as cultural markers, these Latinos would tend to draw on their sense of shared experience as a minority in the United States.
>
> Until now, most public opinion surveys have consistently indicated a fairly weak sense of ethnic Latino identity and a fairly strong sense of nationality. Simply put, people have traditionally opted to identify as Mexican-American, Puerto Rican or other specific national origin over Latino or Hispanic. But as cultures mix

and new generations mature, that may be changing. "For most Latinos these days, nationality doesn't come into play as much unless they just got here," said Tanya Saracho, the Mexican co-founder of the Teatro Luna theater company.

"Mostly we identify as Latinas, American Latinas, whatever that means," Betty Cortina, editor of *Latina* magazine, agreed.

"There's definitely a U.S. based Latino identity," she said. "I identify as Cuban-American because of the place where I was raised (Hialeah, Fla.). But I feel completely connected to Mexican-Americans in Los Angeles and Dominicans in New York, even though we may all have had different experiences."[1]

This U.S.-based Latino identity, which I will refer to as "American or U.S. Latino," is a natural reaction to the rejection we have faced from both parent cultures. We belong to both, yet we belong to neither. In this place of paradox, U.S. Latinos are choosing to continue to identify with their heritage but accept the fact that they are not Latino as defined by our first-generation *puro* brothers and cousins.

I cannot let go of the fact that I have both of these worlds in me and each has left its beautiful and painful mark on me. The challenge for us is to find a way to live in this transitory state of in-between and thrive in it instead of being debilitated by it. For me this can only happen with the support of other second- and third-generation U.S. Latinos who think like me and experience the dissonance that is a part of my daily existence. With them I find clarity and strength for living and flourishing *en mis dos casas* (in my two homes) or as Ed Morales puts it, in a transitory state of in-between:

---

[1]Achy Obejas, "Carving Out a New American Identity: Nationalism Is an Obsolete Idea as Latinos Outgrow Labels," *Chicago Tribune*, September 2, 2001.

At the root of Spanglish [the U.S. Latino experience] is a very universal state of being. It is a displacement from one place, home, to another place, home, in which one feels at home in both place, yet at home in neither place. It is a kind of banging-one's-head-against-the-wall state, and the only choice you have left is to embrace the transitory (read transnational) state of in-between.[2]

THE INEVITABILITY OF CHANGE

Accepting the limitations of living in two cultures is difficult for both our first-generation parents and for those of us who are second- or third-generation. Some of my close first-generation friends are sad that my two young boys, age thirteen and eight at this time of writing, do not speak Spanish well enough to converse with them. I deal with the guilt that perhaps I did not do enough to teach them, that my wife, a fourth-generation Cuban whose grandparents spoke very good English, did not value Spanish enough to push and make them learn. Perhaps we were too lazy or did not value Spanish enough.

At the same time, I am a product of decisions my parents made long ago to leave Puerto Rico for a better life. I do not question whether my parents made the right decision. We have done quite well here in United States, and I am thankful for their love and dedication that made this possible.

Unfortunately, some Latinos do not seem to recognize that with the decision to come to America an eventual loss of language and culture would likely occur. Is this my fault or my son's fault or my parents' fault? To me it is not a question of finding fault; we simply need to accept that Latino identity will look different for succeeding generations, perhaps

---

[2]Ed Morales, *Living in Spanglish: The Search for Latino Identity in America* (New York: St. Martin's Press, 2002), p. 7.

tied less to language than to culture and values instilled in us that intermingle with our new culture in the United States. Language is perhaps the most powerful catalyst for our culture, but it is not the only instrument for retention of Latino culture and identity. I have developed deep internal values and beliefs that I have acquired from my parents but also from my parent culture here in the United States.

Richard Rodriguez is one of the first Latino authors I read who captures the dissonance I felt in my family over issues of language and academics. The very thing Rodriguez's parents encouraged him to do—become a good student and learn English—eventually created distance between himself and those he loved the most. As his English improved and his Spanish skills weakened, he began to feel the weight of disappointment and guilt:

> I recount such incidents only because they suggest the fierce power Spanish had for many people I met at home; the way Spanish was associated with closeness. Most of those people who called me a pocho could have spoken English to me. But they would not. They seemed to think that Spanish was the only language we could use, that Spanish alone permitted our close association. (Such persons are vulnerable always to the ghetto merchant and the politician who have learned the value of speaking their clients' family language to gain immediate trust.) For my part, I felt that I had somehow committed a sin of betrayal by learning English. But betrayal against whom? Not against visitors to the house exactly. No, I felt that I had betrayed my immediate family. I knew that my parents had encouraged me to learn English. I knew that I had turned to English only with angry reluctance. But once I spoke English with ease, I came to feel guilty. (This guilt defied logic.) I felt that

I had shattered the intimate bond that had once held the family close. This original sin against my family told whenever anyone addressed me in Spanish and I responded, confounded.[3]

After reading this during my sophomore year at Colgate University, I was determined to change these feelings of distance from my own family. Whenever I went home to visit my parents, I promised myself, I would speak only Spanish to them as a way to honor them. It was extremely difficult at first, because many thoughts were churning in my head from the intense academic work I was doing. Spanish for me was the language of intimacy and family, not the language through which to express my thoughts and ideas. My Spanish was not strong enough to accomplish that feat. Deciding to live out my Christian values of humility and honoring my parents, I was able to combat the onslaught of alienation that came with achievements in higher education.

But the integration was not complete. I continued to struggle with all I was learning from Western culture versus the values my parents instilled in me. My parents had taught me to be humble. At Colgate you needed a measure of arrogance to convince yourself you could actually achieve high academic excellence. My parents taught me that family was the most important thing. In college I met a group of committed Christians who began to reshape my narrow definition of family to include all those who are believers in Christ. My parents taught me that everything is in God's hands. In college I learned that you determine your own destiny. I experienced the clashing of my two worlds like heavy ivory balls clashing repeatedly on a pool table.

I am very grateful that I disciplined myself to improve my Spanish. My parents were right about the value and power of dominating two lan-

---

[3]Richard Rodriguez, *A Hunger of Meaning* (Boston: Bantam, 1982), p. 30.

guages in a country that is fast becoming Latino. But I live with the knowledge that first-generation, Spanish-dominant Latinos will still judge me based on how well I speak, based on an unwritten rule that to be Latino you must speak Spanish well. Remember Virgilio Elizondo's insight that we as *mestizos* are seen as something less by both parent cultures because we are not perfect mirror images of either. We are seen as a mixture of good and bad, misfits, nonequals.

Yet it is exciting that, as Obejas's article points out, a new Latino identity has been birthed that lies between our two parent cultures. It is a blending of our two cultures, neither and both at the same time. This third culture that conjoins the two with great creativity makes us able to survive and thrive in the United States. I do not want to be all American, just as I don't want to be all Latino. I want them both in me because that is who and what I am. Both-and—together—*en una mezcla* (mixture).

My two sons love to mix drinks together. Often their combinations are terrible, but other times they come up with a combination like orange juice, seltzer, grape juice and apple juice that actually tastes pretty good. That is a good image of what being a U.S. Latino is all about. It is not about being diluted in two cultures but incorporating both with synergism and creativity, like a smooth Latin dance that includes elements from Europe (the French contredans), America (big band jazz) and Africa (rumba).

Some have described this intersection of Latino and American culture as the hyphen in *Hispanic-American,* but a hyphen is not dynamic enough to capture the phenomenon. Ed Morales, author of *Living in Spanglish: The Search for Latino Identity in America,* has found a better term that captures the beauty, complexity and creativity of being Latinos in America:

The working definition for Latinos (or Hispanics) should be "everything." All races, all creeds, all possible combinations.

Then I thought we should call ourselves "Spanglish" because it was a word that expressed what we are doing, rather than where we came from. . . . There is no better metaphor for what a mixed-race culture means than a hybrid language. . . . Spanglish is what we speak, but it is also who we Latinos are, and how we act, and how we perceive the world. . . . The fetishing of pure Spanish only serves a colonial mindset, preventing Latinos from participating in the more dynamic, adaptable world of English. Spanglish is Spanish adapting the crazy rhythms of English, and English inheriting the multicultural content of Latin America. . . . When I speak of Spanglish I'm talking about a fertile terrain for negotiating a new identity.[4]

Growing up, I used Spanglish frequently because there were always technical words or words that I only knew how to say in English. And there were certain phrases or words in Spanish that captured humor or emotion in a way that an English word or phrase could not. In college during a Spanish grammar and composition class our professor asked, "What is the word for 'stuck' in Spanish?" I confidently raised my hand, thinking, *This is easy,* and blurted out, "Estuckiado." I was shocked to find out it was not correct and embarrassed as several White students and my professor laughed at me.

In recent years I have come to embrace Spanglish as part of my Latino experience in this country in spite of the fact that it is frowned on by native speakers who honestly believe that Spanish will be the language spoken in heaven.

---

[4]Morales, *Living in Spanglish*, pp. 3, 7.

When I first began ministry sixteen years ago, I was asked to preach in Spanish during an evening service at a Spanish-speaking Pentecostal church. I was very tempted to speak Spanglish throughout the entire service but knew this would not work for those who used Spanish strictly. I began to get nervous when I realized my entire message would have to be in Spanish. Wishing I could speak perfect Spanish, I kicked myself for all those times in childhood I'd brushed off my mother when she tried to encourage me to speak Spanish more frequently.

As I prepared to leave my apartment and go to the church, it struck me that I could not change who I was. I was a Puerto Rican and an American. My inability to speak impeccable Spanish was part of the package of my Latino experience in this country. I began to reflect on some of the strengths of my experience. For example, that very morning I had addressed a completely White audience and effectively communicated a message of hope in English. I also interacted well with the White pastor and various church leaders. And there I was that very same day preparing to speak to an all Latino audience and in my own choppy way communicate God's truths in Spanish.

Minutes before I was to speak, I wondered how many people sitting in either one of those audiences could have accomplished the same task. Very few, I concluded with a sense of achievement. I took a deep breath and stepped up to the pulpit with renewed courage and self-respect as a U.S. Latino straddling two cultures and languages, comfortable and uncomfortable in my skin all at once.

QUESTIONS FOR REFLECTION AND DISCUSSION

1. If someone were to ask, "What makes someone Latino?" how would your family or friends respond? How would *you* respond to this question?

2. Do you agree that there is such a category as "American or U.S. Latino," a Latino cultural identity based on a common U.S. experience as opposed to national origin? Why or why not?

3. What are some of the factors that link U.S. Latinos together? (For example, marginalization, language and so on.)

4. Living between two cultures can be very challenging at times. Where and when do you find your experience as a Latino most validated?

3

WHERE YOU STAND IN YOUR OWN ETHNIC IDENTITY

If God does have plans to prosper us and give us a hope and a future (Jeremiah 29:11) as U.S. Latinos who are often bilingual, bicultural and biracial, it is important to have some personal insight into our process of forming an ethnic identity. This should not be based on false definitions of what is "Latino enough," since that attitude, as noted in the previous chapter, often ends up excluding and hurting others. Rather, it should be based on what is truly our heritage and on the choices we make to align ourselves with that heritage in the United States.

The Ethnic Identity/Assimilation Grid

Recently my older son, Daniel, was in the hospital for almost three weeks. He had been in a sledding accident so severe it perforated his liver and brought on extensive internal bleeding. Concerned that he was not making progress in an adult intensive care unit in the Bronx, surgeons ordered him transferred by ambulance to the Children's Hospital in Columbia-Presbyterian Hospital Complex in Upper Manhattan. I arrived at the hospital before the ambulance pulled in and was amazed at the size and complexity of this hospital, whose buildings span nearly the entire width of three Manhattan avenues.

In one of the buildings I came to a map so complicated that it was initially quite overwhelming. But then I found a little red dot that showed me exactly where I was at that moment. Now, using the dot as my starting point—and with a bit of direction from a man at the front desk—I could chart out the best route to the Children's Hospital wing. Fortunately, after four months my son Daniel fully recovered. To this day that red dot that helped me find him in a time of desperation and fear remains vivid in my mind.

This chapter presents an ethnic identity grid (figure 1) that can help you see where you stand in your ethnic sense of self. I want to strongly emphasize that this grid is not meant to place judgment. Neither is it meant to make you feel badly about yourself because you are not within the quadrant you or others prefer. It is simply meant to help you clarify where you are. Only then can you determine where you want or need to go in ethnic identity development.

This grid is a map on which you can place a red dot to mark "You Are Here" in your ethnic journey. The grid (adapted from Harry Kitano and Roger Daniels, *Asian Americans: Emerging Minorities*) includes four quadrants, with assimilation as the y-axis and identity as the x-axis. *Assimilation* is the ability to adapt well to the majority culture. It has to do with integrating into schools, workplaces and social gatherings of the majority culture and identifying with it.

We must be careful not to conclude that the only way that someone can adapt well to a culture is by abandoning their own culture. While this is true for some, it is not true for all. I mention this because in certain circles of Latinos, assimilation is seen as a very negative thing because it means you have become *agringado* (acquired cultural traits of Whites).

41

York Moore, an evangelist who has done extensive thinking regarding ethnic identity formation, defines ethnicity as "a group of people sharing a common heritage and manifesting their commonness through their normative trends in their social behavior, work patterns, thought patterns, social tendencies, creative expressions, relation trends and religious perspective." Ethnic identity involves retaining these ethnic ways of thought and behavior.

As you look at the descriptions and try to determine which most pertain to you, keep in mind that they are not fully accurate for everyone. The grid is not scientific but informal and is meant to generate curiosity in those who have not begun to intentionally explore their ethnic self.

After the bullet-point descriptions of each quadrant, I will recommend four steps we all need to take no matter which quadrant we find ourselves in: (1) exploration, (2) appreciation, (3) association and (4) interaction.

Finally, questions are offered to help you make the most of the grid. I recommend that you go through these questions with someone who is able to help you talk about where you stand in regard to assimilation and ethnic identity.

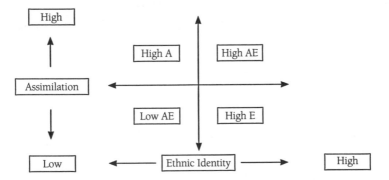

Figure 1. Ethnic Identity/Assimilation Grid, adapted from Harry Kitano and Roger Daniels, *Asian Americans: Emerging Minorities* (Pearson Education, 2000)

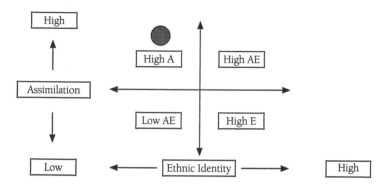

Figure 2. High A (Assimilation): Is able to integrate into majority culture well

Description of High Assimilation

- identifies more as an American (dominant culture) than a Latino
- is likely a third- or fourth-generation Latino
- may speak little if any Spanish
- feels completely at home in the dominant culture
- is more likely to be biracial and have light skin color
- may have grown up and lived in a part of the country with very low numbers of Latinos, isolated from a Latino community
- has likely not made a conscious and intentional choice to identify with her ethnic heritage
- in friendship and social patterns, relates to a high number of non-Latinos
- is more likely to marry a non-Latino
- is likely to associate with Whites, join predominantly White organi-

zations and feel uncomfortable in predominantly Latino settings where Spanish is spoken or Latino culture is emphasized

• may marry a White person without an awareness of cultural factors or the effects this may have in their children

• parents have likely not provided an explanation of or socialization into Latino culture

• may be trying to distance himself from other Latinos and the larger Latino culture and community

• White friends may comment, "We never thought of you as Hispanic"

If you find yourself in this quadrant, it means you have done well at understanding and fitting into the dominant culture in the ways mentioned in the bullet points but have not worked hard at understanding and embracing your ethnic self. If you are committed to growing in your ethnic identity, you will need to take some of the following steps.

1. *Exploration.* Make a decision that you will begin to ask questions about your Latino identity by reading books, taking a class or interacting with other Latinos. Explore the possibility of spending time in your country of origin, another Latin American country or a Latino community in the United States.

2. *Appreciation.* Look for ways in which your ethnic identity is affirmed as a gift from God to bless you and others.

3. *Association.* Make a conscious choice to identify yourself as a Latino, even in situations where it might bring you disapproval from others.

4. *Interaction.* Begin to meet and interact with other Latinos who have a healthy understanding of their culture and can teach you something about yourself.

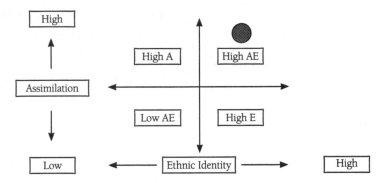

Figure 3. High AE (Assimilation and Ethnicity): Is able to integrate into majority culture and also retain ethnic ways

Description of High Assimilation and Ethnicity

- shows a bicultural perspective in friendship patterns, membership in organizations and the like

- is proud to be able to speak both English and Spanish proficiently, or has a desire and willingness to learn

- is likely a second-, third- or fourth-generation Latino who has grown up in a White neighborhood or has gone to White schools but is still involved in a vibrant Latino community through family, friends, relatives, Latino traditions and holidays

- moves back and forth between American and Latino cultures easily

- is interested in keeping Latino heritage alive and is quite knowledgeable about it

- can serve as a bridge person between cultures

- has had a variety of exposure to both White and Latino contexts and has been affirmed and socialized in both his ethnicity and the dynamics of race relations

- has an understanding of the Latino experience in America and an awareness of some of the current realities her communities face

- can understand and relate to Latino and non-Latino people in healthy, comfortable ways and maintains a strong sense of self in either context

- might easily date or marry a person from any race or ethnicity

- may be involved in a variety of activities and organizations because of her understanding of and commitment to multiethnicity

- is likely to visit his country of origin and interact well with cousins, aunts, uncles and friends of the family

- is able to the see the good and bad of both American and Latino cultures objectively and at times feels both at home with and distant from both cultures

- is likely to view herself as a "U.S. Latina" whose identity is rooted in the dual nature of Latino culture in the United States

If you find yourself in this quadrant, you are in good company with many Latinos, particularly those whose families have been in the United States for generations. High assimilation and identity is a place of real hope and strength but also sadness. As will be discussed in later chapters, *biculturalism* is an ability to exist in two different cultures, enabling us to hold in tension the dualities of our existence as Latinos in the United States. Yet at times we celebrate our ability to adapt to the ambiguity of life, and at other times we grieve over the fact that no matter what we do we can never quite fit in. In *Borderlands: La Frontera,* Gloria Anzaldua says, "The new mestiza copes by developing a tolerance for contradictions, a tolerance for ambiguity. . . . She operates in a pluralistic mode."[1]

---

[1]Gloria Anzaldua, *Borderlands: La Frontera* (San Francisco: Aunt Lute Books, 1987), p. 101.

If you find yourself in this quadrant, you will need to work on the following issues.

1. *Exploration.* Be intentional about exploring ways you can be a bridge person between cultures, to educate, inform and bring wholeness and healing to those in both cultures.

2. *Appreciation.* Begin to see your biculturalism as a place of strength and as an opportunity to thrive in relationships and ministry in a wide assortment of cultural settings.

3. *Association.* Learn Spanish (if you do not speak it well) as a way to strengthen your ability to connect with and care for those in either culture.

4. *Interaction.* Find other "American" Latinos who are living successfully in the tension of both cultures. Be open to talking about your experiences, identifying your strengths, pain and victories, to continue to develop as a bicultural person.

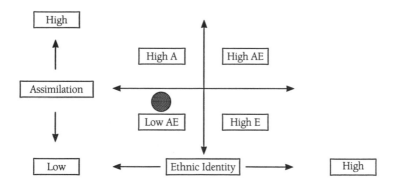

Figure 4. Low AE (Assimilation and Ethnicity): Is unable to integrate into majority culture or retain ethnic ways

Description of Low Assimilation and Ethnicity

- can feel estranged, disenchanted and disillusioned

- may have grown up in the inner city with few quality educational opportunities, unable to become proficient in Spanish *or* English
- is not at home in either of the two cultures
- may be biracial without a strong sense of identity with either race
- may have a deflated sense of ethnic identification
- may not have an understanding of the Latino experience in the United States or an awareness of current realities Latinos face
- is not trying to identify with White culture but also lacks a sense of *orgullo* (pride) in Latino roots and identity
- may have experienced significant racism without the support of a Latino community

Some Latino immigrants may fit in this category if they become isolated from their Latino community and do not speak English well.

If you find yourself in the Low AE quadrant, you very likely experience loneliness, a loss of direction and marginalization beyond what most Latinos feel. To grow toward a healthy sense of Latino identity, it is essential to find others who are able to give you perspective and wisdom for your life.

For those who generally live in a state of low assimilation and low identity, or who find themselves emotionally regressing into this quadrant, I recommend the following specific steps.

1. *Exploration.* Commit yourself to getting to know both the majority culture and your Latino culture. You may want to choose one to focus on for a season of your life. As this is not something you will be able to figure out on your own, you will need to seek out those around you who can help you.

2. *Appreciation.* Ask God to give you an appreciation of your life and

how he has made you. Invite him to guide you as you enter into your journey of self-awareness as a Latino and a child of God.

3. *Association.* Make every effort to avoid isolation. Choose the difficult path of associating with others, trusting that God will bring people into your life who will care for you and give guidance in your ethnic journey.

4. *Interaction.* Try to find a church, ministry or organization that includes Latinos who have had a similar background and life experience to yours, and seek to learn how they have grown toward wholeness.

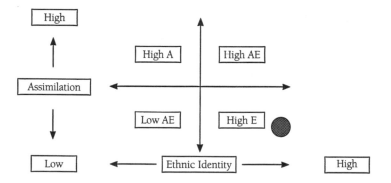

Figure 5. High E (Ethnicity): Is able to retain ethnic ways

Description of High Ethnicity

This category may include newly arrived immigrants who become connected with family or a Latino community.

- identifies more closely with her ethnic culture than with American culture and tends to live with others who have a high sense of ethnic identity

- would likely not refer to himself as "American"
- is more likely a first-generation Latino who prefers speaking Spanish over English
- may have grown up in a predominantly Latino context, perhaps in an urban center, and had few opportunities to interact with majority White culture
- may have adopted this position rather than being socialized into it in childhood
- may have an active dislike or distrust of the dominant culture and institutions
- may have a more honest and balanced understanding of "American" history that has created resentment of Whites or a desire to distance herself from the dominant culture
- is likely to reflect Latino culture in language, tastes, dress and the like
- is not likely to associate with non-Latino people voluntarily
- is not likely to engage in "White" activities such as listening to heavy metal music, playing hockey or watching golf

If you find yourself in the High E quadrant, remember that being able to relate to the dominant culture is an important part of moving forward economically, socially and crossculturally in this country. Some of my friends and family were so committed to Latino purity that they did not bother to learn English well. Others were so frustrated with White racism they refused to associate with them. In the United States it is possible to live in Latino communities and do quite well without speaking a lick of English. However, I believe this is the exception and not the rule. As a whole it will not bring us the greatest opportunities for progress in politics, business or ministry.

I recommend the following ways to grow toward assimilation into the dominant culture in a way that will not undermine your commitment to and love for your culture.

1. *Exploration.* Begin to explore ways to step out of your Latino culture. Do all you can to learn about other cultures, even when you think your approach to something makes more sense. Be willing to explore the possibility that you are ethnocentric (believing that your culture and ethnicity are superior to all others).

2. *Appreciation.* As you learn about non-Latino cultures, ask God to give you an understanding and appreciation for the values, beliefs, traditions and worldview of others. Look for opportunities to learn about and empathize with the oppression and sufferings of others.

3. *Association.* Begin to build crosscultural friendships with people who are willing to openly share their lives with you.

4. *Interaction.* Be willing to step out and meet new people in your job, school or community. Also, be willing to speak out for the needs of others beyond your ethnic group as opportunities arise.

MOVING WITHIN THE GRID

Be careful not to assume that once you are in a certain quadrant of assimilation and ethnic identity, you remain there forever. Because of the dynamics of being Latino in the United States, you may find yourself in a quadrant you thought you had grown out of.

When I am feeling alienated from both cultures as a result of personal failure or someone else's ignorance, I tend to regress to being a Low AE. There are days when I seem to have forgotten who I am as a Latino and am too exhausted physically and emotionally to work at fitting into a majority White setting. These are the days I am most desperate for God's rescue, the support of my White friends and Latino family.

Several years ago I was experiencing racial tension with some of my White colleagues regarding a ministry issue. The emotional trauma was very painful and exhausting. I dropped down from being a High AE to a Low AE in a matter of months. My ability to hold the cultural pieces of my life in balance began to break down. I felt betrayed by members of a majority culture I had invested so much time in, all the while burning bridges that would have led me back to my Latino community for love and support. I entered into a depression that lasted three years. It took me another three years of counseling to unravel the issues of identity that hindered my growth and stunted my leadership.

My healing came as I engaged in and applied the four steps of exploration, affirmation, association and interaction. My initial desire was to seclude myself from others until I was ready to engage once again. However, as I explored the reason for the pain and allowed God to affirm my strengths and gifts, as I continued to associate with Whites in seeking reconciliation in our relationships, and as I interacted with my family and my Latino community in living out who I was with assertiveness and integrity, pent up passivity and anger began to melt away and I was able to engage with others in a healthier way. A sense of clarity and peace steadily flowed back into my mind and my emotions. With greater resolve than before, I chose to pursue what it meant to live out of my ethnic identity not simply for the sake of survival but out of a sense of calling. I am presently learning, once again, to live as a High AE.

In conclusion, I hope this Assimilation/Ethnic Identification Grid will continue to help you explore not only where you stand presently in your ethnic journey but also those areas of your life, be they internal or external, that cause fluctuations or shifts in your understanding of self. Identity development is a complex and dynamic issue we must face with the love and support of a community that knows us and can help us continue to move ahead. As we do so, the payoff will be great: we will experience a sense of wholeness within ourselves, have the maturity and commitment to sustain interracial friendships and pursue shalom (well-being) for others with love and compassion.

QUESTIONS FOR REFLECTION AND DISCUSSION

1. What are the strengths and weaknesses of each quadrant?

2. Where would you place yourself? Why?

3. Which of these do you find yourself moving toward? What help do you need to get there?

4. From a Christian perspective, which of these seems to be closest to where we should be?

5. Based on the quadrant you find yourself in, identify some needs you have for growing in ethnic identity. What resources (people, books, films, magazines, organizations) could be a source of learning and growth for you?

6. Based on the quadrant you find yourself in, what is God teaching you about yourself? Where are you hopeful and where are you discouraged?

7. How can you serve as a catalyst for others to arrive at a healthier place in their ethnic journey?

8. What are the dangers of using this information against another Latino? How can it be misused in a hurtful way?

9. Based on your experience and knowledge, how accurate are these portrayals? What would you add, change or reword?

10. How can these categories be helpful as you interact with others in your workplace, in ministry, in your family?

4

✿

MESTIZAJE:
THE LATINO ETHNIC JOURNEY IN AMERICA

Only a multicultural pueblo can understand
El adentro y the outside of the dynamic
Culturally, we possess ritmos y sueños que no se
Pueden sacar de our essences
They are reflected in our speech and our manner
No matter what language or banner we choose
Freeing us from being aqui o alla, here, there everywhere
Mixed race is the place
It feels good to be neither
It's a relief to deny racial purity
We're amused as America slowly comes to see
The beauty of negritude and the Native American attitude
We've been living it day-to-day since 1492

ED MORALES, "REBIRTH OF NEW RICAN"[1]

---

[1]*el adentro*: "the inside"; *ritmos y sueños que no se pueden sacar de*: "rhythm and dreams that can't be removed from"; *aqui o alla*: "here or there"; *negritude*: "blackness" or "darkness"

We greeted each other with *fuerte abrazo* (strong hugs) as we entered and took our seats in the hotel conference room, excited but also nervous to be together. A small group of young second- and third-generation Latino ministers had gathered for five days of pastoral care and work on Latino identity formation. As we went around the room and had everyone tell why they had come to the conference, a pattern began to develop.

Everyone in the room stated that while they were glad to have come, in some way they didn't feel they belonged there. All of them felt they were not Latino enough, for one reason or another. But none of us could explain what the cutoff point was for being Latino. Some believed that their poor Spanish excluded them; others said that their families had assimilated into mainstream White America, so they didn't grow up in a Latino community. The biracial folks were the most adamant in their discomfort. As "half-breeds," they were convinced they literally were not Hispanic enough.

As the conference progressed we realized that by definition we Latinos are *all* a mixture, descendants of Spaniards, Indians and Africans who mixed willingly or by force. We felt tremendous peace and relief when we discovered that not feeling we belonged is the very thing that defines the Latino experience in America.

Mestizaje (from *mestizo,* "mixed, hybrid") is a paradigm that is very important for understanding the Latino ethnic journey in the Americas. For Latinos to embrace their ethnic identity it is helpful to understand this paradigm and the inferiority instilled in our ancestors that many of us are still plagued with today. In this chapter I want to define *mestizaje* and describe the effect it has had on the Latino psyche historically and more recently. I will also explore ways we can begin to rise above the pain of our *mestizo* roots and allow *mestizaje* to become a basis for pride instead of self-hatred.

WHAT IS *MESTIZAJE*?

But what does this word mean exactly? Virgilio Elizondo and Justo González are two Latino scholars who have written and spoken extensively on the topic of *mestizaje*. Their writing has been very helpful for me in understanding the complexities of the Latino experience. In *Santa Biblia: The Bible Through Hispanic Eyes*, Justo González defines *mestizaje* in this way:

> One of the immediate results of the Spanish conquest of the Western Hemisphere was miscegenation between the Spanish and the Native peoples, whose offspring were called mestizos. Traditionally, this was a pejorative term, by which the Spaniard or the "pure" criollos who were their descendants justified their control of power and wealth, and the oppression of the Indian as well as of the mestizo. A similar process took place with the introduction of slaves from Africa, with the difference that the offspring of white and black parents was called a mulatto—another pejorative term. These words were used pejoratively to such an extent that mestizos themselves, as well as mulattos, often believed that their condition was by nature inferior.[2]

Mestizaje came about through violent means such as conquest, colonization for economic purposes and religious imposition. It also brought with it a new way of looking at life that completely undermined the indigenous worldview, as Virgilio Elizondo writes:

> Beneath the violence of physical conquest there is the deeper violence of the disruption that destroys the conquereds' worldview,

---

[2]Justo González, *Santa Biblia: The Bible Through Hispanic Eyes* (Nashville: Abingdon Press, 1996), p. 77.

which gave cohesion and meaning to their existence. The deepest part of that worldview is the bedrock of the fundamental religious symbol, providing the ultimate rootage of the group's self-identity: the symbols that mediate the absolute. When these symbols are violently destroyed any cohesion for life and meaning of the group is also destroyed.[3]

This kind of spiritual and emotional violence can be more devastating than physical violence. It has power to discredit the identity and worldview of a people. It can also undermine the soul of a culture, leaving nothing to hold on to for meaning in life.

What is also devastating for future generations is to know that both the oppressor and the oppressed are within oneself. It is as if we were suddenly discovering as adults that we were conceived not out of a loving relationship between our mother and father but out of a violent rape. Writing about this harsh history of our ancestors, González reminds us that we live with the fact that our Latino ancestors were not guiltless: "Our Spanish ancestors took the lands of our Indian ancestors. Some of our Indian ancestors practiced human sacrifice and cannibalism. Some of our Spanish forefathers raped our Indian foremothers. Some of our Indian foremothers betrayed their people in favor of the invaders. It is not a pretty story. . . . It is a story resulting in a painful identity."[4]

How does a people recover from such a painful identity resulting from violence? Several historical events and movements began to break this internalized inferiority. The Mexican Revolution affirmed indige-

[3]Virgilio P. Elizondo, *Galilean Journey: The Mexican American Promise* (Maryknoll, N.Y.: Orbis, 1983), p. 10.
[4]Justo González, *Mañana: Christian Theology from a Hispanic Perspective* (Nashville: Abingdon Press, 1990), p. 40.

nous Mexicans and pushed for justice for *mestizos* and Indians in Mexico. Later, mulattos gained pride through a worldwide movement that promoted "negritude" or Black Pride. In *La raza cósmica* Jose Vasconcelos, a Mexican philosopher, laid out a philosophical argument affirming the mixture of races as "the cosmic race"; this brought pride to many Mexican Americans in the late 1920s.[5]

While we have made some progress in affirming our dignity as a people, a deep and subtle sense of inferiority still plagues Latinos that is rooted in the violence, oppression and injustices that is *mestizaje*. When I was young, a *compadre* (close family friend) complained regularly to us that dark-skinned Puerto Ricans were moving into his neighborhood and were going to ruin it because they were loud, disrespectful and didn't take care of their homes. Ironically, he himself was a dark-skinned Puerto Rican, and when he moved into a new home, his White neighbors responded in the same way to his family. Somehow he had internalized racial hatred to such a degree that he had grown to believe his own people were no good and would ruin the neighborhood for him.

I have another friend whose father goes to great lengths to hide his Colombian identity. He has accepted the lies that his people are inferior and evil, that they are all drug-runners who are destroying the fabric of White America. When asked about his ethnicity, he will say that his dad was born in Connecticut and his mother now lives in Vermont. He neglects to mention that his mother and father both grew up in Colombia and that he was born there. His strong English skills and fair skin serve to hide his ethnicity but not his inferiority.

During a conversation about stereotypes Latinos have of each other, a

---

[5]González, *Santa Biblia*, p. 78.

friend of my wife's commented with shame: "My parents [Puerto Rican] always discreetly made snide remarks about how stupid Dominicans were and how prideful Cubans and South Americans were. My brother's wife's family [Ecuadorian] didn't talk to her for a year because they believed she had married a low-class Puerto Rican. My sister-in-law Patricia's father wouldn't even look at my brother Esteban. He would talk to Patricia when he wanted to say something to Esteban or ask him for a favor. He would never address him directly, even if he was in the same room and only a few feet away. The only time he seemed to acknowledge Esteban was when Esteban spoke Spanish. He would laugh *a carcajadas* [uproariously] at every mistake Esteban made, as if to shame and humiliate him."

THE IMPACT OF *MESTIZAJE*

The residual effects of *mestizaje* have created a dynamic that can be toxic. Marginalized people, regardless of their ethnicity and history, develop a pathology of self-hatred that leads to destructive tendencies toward themselves and their own people. Carl Ellis, African American author and lecturer, describes this dynamic as "the crab syndrome." When crabs are placed in a large container, they will climb on top of each other in an effort to get out. Just as the one on top is high enough to climb out, the ones underneath it, desperately trying to get out, yank it down. Fortunately for our stomachs, crabs do not know how to help each other out, and they all end up on our dinner plates. Unfortunately for us, oppressed people often claw at each other instead of realizing who is truly creating havoc and trying to devour them.

We see the crab syndrome even in the Scriptures. In Exodus 2:11-14 Moses goes out to be with his people. He sees two Hebrews fighting each other and decides to stop them. Moses knows he is an Israelite. In stopping the fight he is reaching out to help his people and identifying with his true ethnicity as a Hebrew. He pulls them apart and asks the one who started it, "Why are you hitting your fellow Hebrew?"

But something very strange happens. The Hebrew speaks harshly and disrespectfully to Moses, who at that time is still part of Pharaoh's household and therefore royalty. To speak so harshly to someone of the royal Egyptian family meant swift and sudden death.

The aggressive Israelites spoke to him in such a manner because they knew he was a Hebrew. Moses had killed an Egyptian who was brutalizing a fellow Hebrew, and they used this fact against him. Like crabs clawing at each other, they wanted to bring Moses down with them. They did not thank him for protecting them when no one else would stand up against their oppression. Instead they put fear in him and resented him for being a fellow Hebrew.

OUR NEED FOR GOD AND OTHERS

Understanding byproducts of *mestizaje* such as self-hatred and low sense of self-worth has helped me come to terms with my own struggles with inferiority. Negative thoughts about myself are always with me, lurking behind every new way, ready to pounce just as I am about to trust God in a new way. Writing this book has been an exercise in trusting God to dismantle the lies that sneak up to overwhelm me. Learning to play the drums at the age of thirty-seven was also a step of trust because I thought I had lost my window of opportunity as a child.

To have a healthy perspective on being Latino is an act of faith. Our blood is from a mixture that was viewed negatively from the very beginning of our people's history. This is not something you just deal with and move on from, because it eats at the soul of a people. It is something to

look at and ponder and surrender daily to God in an act of obedience.

But it is also something we must embrace as our reality as we see the strengths of our *mestizo* roots. Elizondo articulates well the flip side of *mestizaje*: "To be an insider-outsider, as is the mestizo, is to have closeness to and distance from both parent cultures. A mestizo people can see and appreciate characteristics in its parent cultures that they see neither in themselves nor in each other. It is threatening to be in the presence of someone who knows us better than we know ourselves."[6]

What is most interesting about *mestizaje* is that it is not just something that occurred to our ancestors centuries ago; it is a process that is with us today. At the beginning of this chapter I told about a conference in which all of us who attended, especially the biracial Latinos, felt as if we did not belong. Had they known more about the Latino *mestizaje* dynamic, they would have realized that in them another level of *mestizaje* had taken place. As González says, "A Mexican-American is the result of a double *mestizaje*: first, of Indian and Spanish, to produce the Mexican; second, of Mexican and North American, to produce the Mexican-American."[7] To presume that your *mestizaje* rules you out of the choice to identify with your Latino heritage is false, because it is your *mestizo* roots that mark you as a Latino.

What does this mean then for us as American Latinos? Do we give up and grow more and more bitter at our plight? Should we pity ourselves and create good excuses to explain why we cannot do the things we long to do?

I am seeing more and more windows of opportunity where the pain and ugliness of my *mestizo* (actually mulatto) roots can serve as an advantage rather than handicap. My background has created in me com-

---

[6]Elizondo, *Galilean Journey*, p. 18.
[7]González, *Santa Biblia*, p. 80.

passion for others throughout the world who experience oppression and injustice. It has given me greater love for and commitment to other Latinos. In my family it has given me great patience and wisdom. I have chosen to rise up above my painful roots, not in my own strength but in humility turning to a God who understands my history better than I do and is helping me to see the purposes and destiny for my life. God has a way of taking what others despise and through it bringing liberation and hope. I must choose each day to live under God's ongoing redemption in my life rather than under the weight of inferiority that I have internalized through my *mestizo* roots.

As I look back on that conference of Latino campus pastors, I am grateful for the gift of clarity and insight God had given us regarding our Latino ethnic selves. We hadn't fully understood the source of our pain, yet we knew that at this point in our lives only we could comfort and support one another. We entered the hotel conference room alone and hesitant and departed together, embraced in tears, laughter and cheerfulness as if a heavy load had been lifted off our shoulders. We had found a piece of ourselves in each other, and it was worth celebrating. For a brief moment we could feel as if we completely belonged: we could live in our *mestizo* skin and just be. Something that was broken deep down in our hearts had begun to get fixed as we learned more about ourselves and encountered God with those who were most like us in almost every way: confused *mestizos* in an unforgiving and unwelcoming world.

QUESTIONS FOR REFLECTION AND DISCUSSION

1. How can an understanding of your history and the paradigm of *mestizaje* be helpful in developing your sense of ethnic identity?

2. Try to identify negative traits that your family passed on to you. They

may include emotional, spiritual or psychological patterns such as fear of success, self-hatred, fear of authority, apathy.

3. Have you struggled with issues of inferiority? How might these feelings be tied to being Latino or Latina? What has helped you overcome these feelings?

4. How have other Latinos been a source of strength and encouragement to you as you have identified with your ethnic roots?

5

❀

ETHNICITY
IN THE SCRIPTURES

*One of the more fascinating proposals which has been made
in theological discussions of the biblical notion of "the image of
God" is that this image has a "corporate" dimension. That is,
there is no one human individual or group who can fully bear or
manifest all that is involved in the image of God so that there
is a sense in which that image is collectively possessed. The
image of God is, as it were, parceled out among the peoples of
the earth. By looking at different individuals and groups we get
glimpses of different aspects of the full image of God.*

RICHARD MOUW, *WHEN THE KINGS COME MARCHING IN*

Anything that we tack on to the gospel has the potential to become idol-
atrous. But what is the gospel? It is the good news that Jesus has come
into the world to liberate everyone of every ethnicity, whether Jew or
Gentile, Roman or Korean, Black or Latino, from sin and death through
the exchange of his own life on the cross so that we might live in the forgiveness and love of the Father. The apostle Paul as he begins his letter

to the Romans makes it clear that the power of God for our salvation lies in this good news in the context of our ethnic particularities: "I am not ashamed of the gospel, because it is the power of God for the salvation of everyone who believes: first for the Jew, then for the Gentile" (Romans 1:16).

This chapter will offer a biblical framework for ethnic culture. A fresh look at the lives of Moses, Esther, Mordecai, Jesus and Paul will make clear that our ethnic identity can be a tool in the hands of God to fulfill his purposes in the world.

FROM THE BEGINNING

The creation reveals that humanity was made in the image of God. We were made to be in relationship with one another just as God is in relationship with himself in the Trinity. We were created with the ability to reason and with the propensity to be creative. We were also given a mandate to "fill the earth and subdue it" (Genesis 1:28). Reformed theologians have termed this "the cultural mandate." Richard Mouw describe this cultural mandate as follows:

> God intended from the beginning that human beings would "fill the earth" with the processes, patterns, and products of cultural formation. . . . The command to "fill" the earth here is not merely a divine request that Adam and Eve have a lot of babies. The earth was also to be "filled" by the broader patterns of their interactions with nature and with each other. . . . To "subdue" the Garden would be to transform untamed nature into a social environment.[1]

Culture, then, was not a warped, distorted byproduct of the Fall but

---

[1]Richard Mouw, *When the Kings Come Marching In* (Grand Rapids: Eerdmans, 1983), pp. xv, 16.

was part of the created order in the Garden, and God saw it was "very good" (Genesis 1:26-31). As the first human beings developed particular ways of tilling the soil, for example, the first culture began to take shape.

It was when Adam and Eve succumbed to sin that all things, including this cultural mandate, suddenly became susceptible to distorted effects of the Fall (Genesis 3:17). Not only was the ground cursed, but Romans 8:20-22 makes it clear that all of creation has since groaned with pain and longing for freedom: "The creation waits in eager expectation for the sons of God to be revealed. For the creation was subjected to frustration, not by its own choice, but by the will of the one who subjected it, in hope that the creation itself will be liberated from its bondage to decay and brought into the glorious freedom of the children of God."

In an early attempt of human beings to bring their own restoration, they joined together to build a tower that would bring them fame and unity. "Now the whole world had one language and a common speech. . . . Then they said, 'Come, let us build ourselves a city, with a tower that reaches to the heavens, so that we may make a name for ourselves and not be scattered over the face of the whole earth'" (Genesis 11:1, 4). But God intervened and prevented this unity from occurring. He viewed their oneness in language and purpose as evil. He chose to scatter them throughout the earth, where a diversity of ethnic cultures with different languages could form. This scattering was not a form of punishment but rather a protection for them, preventing them from trying to gain a unity and a name without reference to God. Here God is acting on his intent to return humankind to its cultural mandate to fill the earth and not simply remain in one geographical area. In his book *Living in Color: Embracing God's Passion for Diversity*, Randy Woodley states, "God has planned since the beginning of time to cultivate diversity among human beings. When people tried to circumvent His plan, God intervened by creating many languages. Distinctions would have developed naturally over time, and changes would undoubtedly have taken place anyway if the people had spread out and obeyed God. His intervention merely sped up the process of developing the various ethnic groups that brought about His intended diversity."[2]

MOSES, A MAN OF ETHNIC PASSION

Throughout the Scriptures we find God affirming culture with the intent of bringing all cultures and peoples under his lordship, as opposed to merging them all into a homogenous culture. Let us now turn our attention to various characters in the Scriptures who took their ethnic culture seriously and honored God through them. In Exodus 2 we see that Moses, even though he had been raised in an Egyptian home, was very aware of his ethnic roots. When Moses saw an Egyptian brutalize a fellow Israelite (Exodus 2:11), he could not hold back his outrage. Moses identified with his people and was appalled at their mistreatment by the Egyptians. Scripture does not tell us, but it is likely that Moses had gone out to see his people on other occasions. It is also likely that he had seen this kind of abuse before and had had enough. In the heat of the moment when no Egyptian was looking, Moses killed the abusive Egyptian. Such an extreme act showed how torn Moses must have been in trying to come to terms with his Egyptian culture and his Jewish ethnicity.

Moses had done a terrible thing, but it was out of righteous indignation. Moses' passion for his people burned in his blood to the extent that he was willing to risk everything to protect one of his own.

---

[2]Randy Woodley, *Living in Color: Embracing God's Passion for Diversity* (Grand Rapids: Baker, 2001), p. 21.

Some years later, God called him:

> The LORD said, "I have indeed seen the misery of my people in
> Egypt. I have heard them crying out because of their slave drivers,
> and I am concerned about their suffering. So I have come down to
> rescue them from the hand of the Egyptians and to bring them up
> out of that land into a good and spacious land, a land flowing with
> milk and honey—the home of the Canaanites, Hittites, Amorites,
> Perizzites, Hivites and Jebusites. And now the cry of the Israelites
> has reached me, and I have seen the way the Egyptians are op-
> pressing them. So now, go. I am sending you to Pharaoh to bring
> my people the Israelites out of Egypt." (Exodus 3:7-10)

We Christians today would certainly not have written the script this way;
in our eyes God does not use ungodly, violent men to accomplish his
will. Yet somehow, whether it was at an early age or as an adult, Moses
showed concern for his people and responded, albeit inappropriately, by
murdering an Egyptian as he tried to defend one of his own people.

God had placed a longing in Moses' heart to be a defender of God's
people. His strong ethnic awareness could be put to good use to bring
about their freedom. At this point Moses' ethnic identity as an Israelite
was not fully developed, but as he obeyed God and returned to confront
the powers of Egypt, God matured him as an Israelite who would be accepted by his own people as their spokesman. Moses also developed his
confidence in God as he saw God at work. What began in Moses' act of
angry violence matured into a life of obedience through which God
would launch his plan of deliverance for Israel.

I can relate well with Moses' development because there are parallels
in my own life. God slowly but surely instilled in me a strong sense of
ethnic identification. His purpose was not simply to make me a more

whole person but to raise me up as a leader who would bring the gospel to Latinos in need of salvation, hope and liberation. When I see Latinos mistreated and marginalized, something rises deep within me to seek justice. I cannot sit and passively watch Latinos being abused, neglected and discriminated against.

However, I am recognizing that this longing for justice must be applied beyond my ethnic group. It must encompass anyone in need, because God is concerned for all people who are unjustly treated. And he calls us to love the world as he does.

Several years ago I became the national director of InterVarsity's Latino Fellowship. Perhaps initially I took the position with a desire to enjoy greater personal recognition. However, I believe now my motives are lining up more closely with God's motives. The purpose for my connection with my Latino identity was to ensure that within the ministry of Inter-Varsity the needs of Latino students would not be ignored or overlooked.

For many years as a result of poor planning and strategy and a reluctance to change, InterVarsity had unintentionally neglected Latino students. We suffered from what Manuel Ortiz calls a fear of destructuring. God must raise up leaders who will challenge the way things have always been done particularly in our religious institutions so that those on the margins can be reached, says Ortiz:

> I am working with various organizations and denominations. I have found that they have to destructure, and the moment I start to talk about their need to destructure before they restructure, nobody wants to talk about it, because to radically change as an institution is too much work and there's too much pain involved.[3]

---

[3]Manuel Ortiz, personal interview, March 1, 2003.

InterVarsity was oriented toward ministry on residential campuses, whether private colleges or large state universities. Here our strategy for campus outreach was quite effective. Unfortunately, it meant the neglect of most Latino and Black students, who tend to be at urban commuter schools or community colleges, places where our campus strategies were least effective. That is not to say that InterVarsity did nothing for Latino and Black students. I myself am a product of InterVarsity. In my later ministry I worked at urban commuter schools in New York City for many years, reaching out to Black and Latino students. However, I and a small number of others were the exception.

Now that I have been placed in a position to speak for the needs of Latino staff and students, God is deepening in me a greater sense of ethnic self for his purposes. I am seeing that it goes far beyond me to the heart of what God is doing in our nation as the number of Latinos grows exponentially. I see my role and the role of a growing number of Latino leaders in mostly White religious institutions as the first stage of great changes that must come if God's justice is to prevail in the life of the Latino community in America.

Moses did not know what God had in store for him. He simply followed his instincts to defend and protect his people, and God transformed them for good. I do not know what God has in store for me; I am simply moving forward and following my instincts. I trust that my instincts for pursuing a strong sense of ethnic self will bear fruit for the kingdom as I seek to obey Christ. May my obedience serve as a good instrument in the hands of God, who uses all that we are to rescue the lives of those desperate for his help.

MORDECAI AND ESTHER: FOR SUCH A TIME AS THIS

Esther, who happened to be Jewish, became queen in the Persian empire after Queen Vashti displeased King Xerxes. Mordecai, Esther's cousin who had adopted her as his own daughter, emphasized to her that she should hide her ethnic identity as an Israelite: "But Esther had kept secret her family background and nationality just as Mordecai had told her to do, for she continued to follow Mordecai's instructions as she had done when he was bringing her up" (Esther 2:20). One might conclude prematurely that Mordecai was ashamed of his identity as an Israelite and passed his shame on to Esther. Mordecai's initial motive was to protect Esther in a society that was hostile to Jews. It is what any loving father who sensed danger for his daughter would do.

Later Mordecai uncovered and helped to foil a plot to assassinate King Xerxes. Afterward, Haman, one of the king's nobles, was elevated to the highest seat of honor instead of Mordecai, and when Mordecai refused to pay obeisance to him, Haman plotted to not only kill Mordecai but also annihilate his people throughout the entire kingdom of Xerxes.

When Mordecai learned of the scheme to harm him and his people, he tore his clothes, put on sackcloth and ashes and went out into the city wailing loudly and bitterly. Then, realizing the possibility of extinction of his people, he took action. The only one who could save his people now was King Xerxes, and the only one who could go before the king to speak out for her people was Esther. It was time for his daughter to reveal her true ethnic identity and help the Jews escape genocide.

Mordecai filled Esther with a vision for her people and an understanding of the providence and faithfulness of God. He called on her to take a risk on behalf of her people:

Do not think that because you are in the king's house you alone of all of the Jews will escape. For if you remain silent at this time, relief and deliverance for the Jews will arise from another place, but you and your father's family will perish. And who knows but that you have come to royal position for such a time as this? (Esther 4:13-14)

Mordecai was distressed by the potential destruction of his people, and he realized that if Esther continued to hide her identity, she would miss out on the opportunity to serve as God's vessel for the rescue of her people. He convinced her that her beauty, her ethnic identity as a Jew and her strategic placement as queen were the work of God for the salvation of her people. Fortunately, Esther listened to Mordecai and saw God's miraculous intervention through her obedience and willingness to die for the sake of her people.

> "If I have found favor with you, O king, and if it pleases your majesty, grant me my life—this is my petition. And spare my people—this is my request. For I and my people have been sold for destruction and slaughter and annihilation. If we had merely been sold as male and female slaves, I would have kept quiet, because no such distress would justify disturbing the king."
> King Xerxes asked Queen Esther, "Who is he? Where is the man who has dared to do such a thing?"
> Esther said, "The adversary and enemy is this vile Haman." (Esther 7:3-6)

This story teaches us about God's faithfulness. In this instance his faithfulness came through a father and a daughter who were driven by a deep sense of belonging to a people and knowing that God was at work through their ethnic identification.

As we mature in our ethnic identity, it is vital to grow in spiritual depth that can sustain and nurture us. Only then will we be placed "for such a time," a season of great opportunity to help meet the needs of our people and the needs of others God moves our hearts to love. We are to be defenders of all people who are treated unjustly—the poor and the oppressed of the world.

As the stories of both Moses and Esther make clear, God often brings deliverance to a people through someone who is part of that people group. Who would have more motivation and commitment to bring God's righteousness and justice to an oppressed people than those within that very community?

We can and must lay our ethnic identity—along with everything else—at God's feet with a hopeful expectancy that there is much work to be done under the leadership of a God who is faithful to all.

JESUS THE JEW

Jesus was not acultural or nonethnic. The Son of God was incarnated into a specific culture. He recognized and adhered to many cultural guidelines and boundaries, even though he was always stretching them. For instance, Jesus honored his Father by keeping the Sabbath. He did challenge rules about the kinds of activities that were permissible on the Sabbath; his actions of healing were mistakenly interpreted as failures to keep the Sabbath, but these were mistaken judgments.

When Jesus turned water into wine at the wedding at Cana in Galilee (John 2), he was upholding certain values that were important to the Jewish people. It was customary to provide wine throughout the entire wedding reception, even if it was bad wine. The wine had run out before the festivities were over. Mary, Jesus' mother, knew that this would be a source of great embarrassment for the family and the newlyweds. Having spent much of her life pondering the signs of her son's divinity, she turned to him for help. Jesus suggested that doing this favor could compromise his heavenly mission because it was not yet his time to be revealed. Yet he took this opportunity to reveal his glory to his disciples—in a way that honored his mother and the cultural context of the moment.

In this one miraculous act he showed not only his divinity but also his humanity and the value he placed on ethnic identity. He knew the value of culture and chose to live out the full extent of his humanity within it. How could Jesus be fully human if he did not live within the dictates of culture and ethnicity?

Jesus knew the place of the Pharisees, the priests and the Sadducees and their roles in the life of the community. He often sent those he healed to these leaders so that they could be officially pronounced cured and clean based on Jewish customs and religious requirements. On one occasion we find Jesus directing ten men with leprosy, "'Go, show yourselves to the priests.' And as they went, they were cleansed" (Luke 17:14). As they obeyed Jesus and began to walk by faith, Jesus cured them. His purpose here was to test their faith and to heal them—but to do so with respect to the cultural and religious customs of the time. He did not tell them to simply walk and be healed, but to go and be healed *and* restored rightfully into the community through the culturally prescribed means, the pronouncement of the priest. Again, in this account Jesus' divinity is evident in the context of his human culture and ethnicity.

JESUS' INCARNATION

Christ took on the full extent of humanity when he was born without losing any of his divinity. Although he was without sin, he still experienced the pain and destructiveness of others' sin. While on earth Jesus was in perfect communion with creation. His miracles showed the perfect relationship between his divinity and his humanity: he liberated creation as he went along. Jesus had two natures in one person. He was not partly or occasionally God or human; he was both at all times.

> Since the children have flesh and blood, he too shared in their humanity so that by his death he might destroy him who holds the power of death—that is, the devil—and free those who all their lives were held in slavery by their fear of death. For surely it is not angels he helps, but Abraham's descendants. For this reason he had to be made like his brothers in every way, in order that he might become a merciful and faithful high priest in service to God, and that he might make atonement for the sins of the people. Because he himself suffered when he was tempted, he is able to help those who are being tempted. (Hebrews 2:14-18)

Jesus came and lived with us and became like us in every way so that he could become our mediator before the Father. If it is true that humans by nature acquire values, traits, behaviors and all that encompasses culture and ethnicity, then we must conclude that ethnicity and culture are something Jesus acquired, lived with, struggled with, was blessed by and engaged in. Scripture says that he was made to be like his brothers and sisters in every way, including ethnic identity and culture.

Why is it then that we are quick to conclude that ethnicity is not important? Why do we see it as a threat to diversity? And why do we not invite Jesus to enter into our cultures and redeem them so that the true richness of each is brought forth?

> Since we have a great high priest who has gone through the heavens, Jesus the Son of God, let us hold firmly to the faith we profess. For we do not have a high priest who is unable to sympathize with our weaknesses, but we have one who has been tempted in every way, just as we are—yet was without sin. Let us then approach the

throne of grace with confidence, so that we may receive mercy and find grace to help us in our time of need. (Hebrews 4:14-16)

Besides knowing that Jesus' full humanity means he can identify with our sufferings, what gives me the greatest encouragement is knowing that Jesus Christ's own lineage was mixed. Justo González writes:

> Mestizaje, both genetic and cultural, is part of the biblical reality, even though the deuteronomist historian may have tried to suppress it. In writing his Gospel, Matthew could well have tried to suppress Jesus' own mestizaje—he was, after all, the "son of David" come to claim David's throne. Instead, of the four women mentioned in his genealogy, two are Gentiles. Therefore, as followers of the mestizo Jesus, we shall learn to read the Bible, and life itself, as mestizos who have much to offer.[4]

PAUL, THE CULTURAL *MESTIZO*

Paul is a New Testament character whose zeal for his people is admirable. In fact, we are all too familiar with the zealous, ruthless ways he persecuted the first Christians in the name of protecting his religion and his people from this strange sect. As God called Moses, we find God calling out Paul in all of his zealousness. Once Paul had been converted, it was his zeal that God used to transform the world, taking the gospel to the entire known world through Paul's missionary journeys. He was certainly not ashamed of the gospel, nor was he ashamed of his Jewishness.

God used the full extent of Paul's identity—not only as a Jew but also as a Roman citizen—to advance the gospel across the world:

> The fact of the matter is that Saul, like many others in his time, had

---

[4]Justo González, *Santa Biblia: The Bible Through Hispanic Eyes* (Nashville: Abingdon, 1996), p. 90.

two names, *Saul and Paul.* He was named Saul after the great leaders of his own tribe of Benjamin. But he had also a Roman name, a name for use outside of Jewish circles. That name was Paul. Saul/ Paul was a cultural mestizo, as were many of his contemporaries. As long as Saul/Paul is in a basically Jewish environment, Luke refers to him as Saul. Now, as he begins his mission to the Gentiles, and at the precise moment when Saul is about to give his first witness before a Gentile, Luke, almost offhandedly, refers to Saul, also known as Paul. If there is a difference between Saul and Paul, that difference does not revolve around the experience on the road to Damascus, but around his mission to the Gentiles.[5]

Just as God used Paul's dual identity to advance the gospel to Jews and Romans, I hope that many Latinos will see the benefit of their dual identity and speak into the strengths and deficiencies of both cultures. Our journey is about taking the strengths of each culture to the other, so that God is honored in both of them. Ultimately our goal should be that we are willing to be all things to all people, as Paul clearly stated in the Scriptures, in order for God's salvation to unfold in everyone's lives.

To conclude, I have tried to present a biblical framework for ethnicity and culture. I have also tried to demonstrate how God utilized the ethnic identity of specific biblical characters to accomplish his work in the world. Moses, Esther, Mordecai, Jesus and Paul became willing vessels who lived out of the strengths of their ethnic identity and cultural context and eventually fulfilled God's call on their lives.

QUESTIONS FOR REFLECTION AND DISCUSSION

1. What Scriptures have helped inform you about the value of culture?

---

[5]Ibid., p. 81.

2. Are there ways God has used your ethnicity to affect the lives of others in your ethnic group?

3. How can God use your ethnic identity to be a blessing to others outside your ethnic group?

4. How does Jesus' own humanity affirm us in our pursuit of ethnic identity?

5. How are you able to relate to Moses, Esther, Mordecai, Jesus or Paul?

6. Are there other biblical characters who lived out of the context of their culture and ethnicity? Who are they and what can we learn from them?

6

❀

CHRISTIAN FAITH AND ETHNIC CULTURE

It is my judgment, therefore, that we should not make it difficult for the Gentiles who are turning to God. Instead we should write to them, telling them to abstain from food polluted by idols, from sexual immorality, from the meat of strangled animals and from blood.

ACTS 15:19-20

God is colorblind. He doesn't see our color, race or ethnicity." I heard these words from a friend who invested in my early Christian life. He would say earnestly, "When we become Christians, our identity has to come from our new relationship with Jesus and the family of God. Nothing else really matters. Look at Paul's life. He counted everything as dung for the gospel."

I respected my friend and valued his opinion, but something in his words did not sit well with me. The more I thought about it, the more I was convinced that God did care about every dimension of my life.

This chapter posits that our ethnic identity is something we cannot avoid. Therefore, we should offer it to God and invite him to redeem this important part of us. In fact, God cares deeply about our ethnic identity and even celebrates it with us.

I want to be clear, though, that culture and ethnicity are not to be set over and above who we are in Christ. My greatest joy is that I now belong to the family of God and that I am coheir with Christ. The most significant mark on my life is that I am a follower of the one true God and his Son Jesus Christ. I try to let these truths inform all that I do.

Yet I come to Christ in a cultural context, no matter how hard I may try to avoid or deny this reality. Manuel Ortiz, professor of practical theology at Westminster Theological Seminary, reminds us that only God has no culture or ethnicity: "Only God is supracultural or above culture. Anyone who doesn't see themselves as having an ethnicity is claiming to be universal, which leads to an attitude of superiority. This is very problematic."[1]

SEPARATING FAITH AND ETHNICITY

Why do some Christians insist that our faith and ethnicity have to be separated? Denise Cuesta, a second-generation Nuyorican (a Puerto Rican raised in New York City) who is worship director at New Life in the Bronx Church, recalls the difficult challenges of growing up in a Spanish Pentecostal home. Her father, who served as pastor, wanted nothing to do with his culture; he believed it would get in the way of growing in Christ. Following is a large portion of an interview I had with Mrs. Cuesta that I believe epitomizes the emotional effects of separating faith from ethnicity. Often it takes years to recapture what was lost when our ethnic identity is stripped from our faith.

---

[1]Manuel Ortiz, personal interview, March 2003.

Denise Cresta: I don't think that I had a typical Puerto Rican upbringing, because I was born and raised Protestant. I always felt
different from other Latinos because of the Catholic tradition. I
grew up in a strict Pentecostal upbringing. I couldn't wear jewelry,
I couldn't cut my hair or anything.

Orlando Crespo: How did that happen? What was your religious
family history?

DC: My father's family was Methodist in Puerto Rico, from a long
line of Methodists. My mother was Catholic, but she converted
when she met my father. When he came from Puerto Rico to New
York, he went to the Methodist church, but the style of worship
wasn't charismatic, so he went to a Pentecostal church where he
adopted a legalistic frame of mind.

When I went to school, I felt really different because of the way
I dressed. And when they found out that my father was a pastor,
they assumed he was a priest. I decided that I just wouldn't discuss
it because it was too confusing and created a lot of problems for me.

My upbringing was not full of the typical Latino dancing. Since
music and revelry were considered sinful, I was never taught about
my culture other than food. History was never discussed unless it
was in a derogatory way. I grew up thinking that there was something wrong with my culture. Even when I became an adult and I
knew differently, I still believed that wanting to be in tune with my
culture was wrong and sinful.

OC: So you don't remember it ever being discussed in church or
in sermons?

DC: There was a joke the people in the church would say: when we get to heaven, we will all discover that the "heavenly language" is Spanish. That was the only time they talked about having pride in their culture. Often, when we did talk about our culture, it would end up being a discussion about Santería [a voodoo-like religion] and how evil it was. The best thing to do was to not try and find out about your culture.

OC: What else turned you away from getting connected with your ethnicity and culture?

DC: The major thing was the feeling that my culture was sinful. It was wrong to try to be cultural or to try to bring my cultural perspective into my faith. Christianity had to be separate from all of that or somehow above all of that. Culture was worldly and Christianity was heavenly.

During last year's Thanksgiving celebration, members of my husband's family were teaching my daughter how to dance salsa. I realized I never had that and felt the void, a sense of loss of never having had it. I had never been allowed to feel a sense of belonging not only to God's family but to my Latino community. I missed the sense of the strong Latino family unit, the ties and the acceptance of extended family.

OC: As you have begun to explore your ethnic identity, what discoveries have you made regarding the relationship between your faith and your ethnic identity?

DC: A book called *Diverse Worship: African-American, Caribbean and Hispanic Perspectives* by Petrito Maynard-Reid has begun to open up a whole new way of worshiping God through my culture. I am discovering that if I don't know who I am in the context of culture, then I don't really know who I am. That has to affect my relationship with God. I have adopted ways of thinking and attitudes that are in line with majority White culture instead of Latino culture. For example, in the past I was very resistant to using dance as a form of worship because I did not see it emphasized in the White church.

But for Caribbeans worship is very expressive. The book helped me to realize that my resistance to dance as a form of worship was just a reflection of my background in White Christian culture, not any deep spiritual conviction that dance was wrong; it was a cultural resistance. It didn't have a scriptural basis but was more about me feeling uncomfortable about it. At the same time, I didn't want to get lost in the culture of it all but wanted the truth.

I've also started doing hymns at church because I wanted to incorporate all forms of worship. All of it is of God. All the peoples, cultures and customs reflect something of God. He is so infinite that it takes the entire population of the world to reflect him. I want the worship at New Life in the Bronx church to have African roots, Hispanic and European flavors, though some people may feel uncomfortable about it.

OC: But that will be their starting point and an opportunity to grow. That's what church is all about: making people feel uncomfortable so they can be stretched and trust God in new ways.

As you look at Scripture, has it helped you to say to yourself, "It's OK to get in touch with my ethnic identity"?

DC: I can't think of any specific Scripture right now. It has been a slow and gradual awakening starting from my own general dissatisfaction with the way things were and my expressions toward

God, the ways I relate to people, my family and culture. I had started to feel that there had to be more than what I had been experiencing from my childhood growing up. Living in a poor Jamaican neighborhood right now and looking at the crime rate and the economic disadvantages that are all around me, and then realizing that in a span of four blocks there are four churches, has gotten me thinking that there's got to be more of an answer than just attending church.

The gospel has to be more than this one-dimensional spiritual life. I can't assume anymore that God's not interested in what I do and how I live. That has pushed me to start questioning about culture. How do I take what I believe to be the truth and bring it to where I live? It has to be more than assuming we are going to solve all the problems of the world by starting a church and setting people free spiritually without touching their physical needs. That is just the beginning. As a church we have to reach out. We are talking about culture, economics, things that don't sound spiritual. It has to impact that or else it's useless. I believe in political Christianity. We have to take it out of the church and bring it to where people live. It has to effect political and social change.[2]

Echoing Denise's experience growing up in the church, I do not recall ever hearing a strong message that affirmed my Latino ethnicity in my Catholic church or the Protestant churches I attended later in life. The perception was always that pursuing a sense of ethnic self would compete with my faith and eventually turn me away from God, because I would take it to an extreme and become obsessed with it. The fear was that I would become ethnocentric, caring only about my people and culture.

---

[2]Denise Cuesta, personal interview, March 2003.

In our pursuit of God anything that we place before loving and honoring him alone can become an idol. Some people find themselves ethnically and abandon everything else, including God. Anything we value has the potential to consume our thoughts and our time in unhealthy and even destructive ways. But it is also possible to value things in such a way that they hold a healthy and necessary place in our lives. Ethnicity has the potential to enrich our life with Christ and nurture our respect of cultures different than our own.

Many Americans fear emphasizing their cultural identity because this might lead to tribalism, a condition in which you care about and fight for only the issues that affect your group at the expense of others in need. A healthy ethnic identity should actually lead to a *greater* appreciation for the differences of others, because you know how valuable your own distinctiveness is. Only in an environment where people are encouraged to pursue a healthy ethnic identity is diversity possible, since diversity is about equally affirming all the cultures and ethnicity that are present. Unity through monoculturalism is our enemy, because all too often it is the majority culture that wins out, cutting everyone off from true diversity. Healthy diversity can be used by God to bring affirmation, wholeness and life to all.

DEFINING CULTURE

In a 1978 report by the Lausanne Committee for World Evangelization, *The Willowbank Report on Gospel and Culture,* culture was defined as

> an integrated system of beliefs (about God or reality or ultimate meaning), of values (about what is true, good, beautiful and normative), of customs (how to behave, relate to others, talk, pray, dress, work, play, trade, farm, eat, etc.) and of institutions which

express these beliefs, values and customs (government, law courts, temples or churches, family, schools, hospitals, factories, ships, unions, clubs, etc.) which bind a society together and give it a sense of identity, dignity, security and continuity.[3]

As human beings it is impossible to live outside of these integrated systems of belief, values, customs and institutions, for they give us the connectedness and belonging that are essential to the human heart. It is in this environment of culture that God gives us the sense of identity and dignity that are necessary for physical, emotional and mental wholeness. It is culture that frames all that we do and guides our steps as we dance the steps of life together.

In a multicultural environment like the United States we are fortunate to have many cultures that exist within our larger American culture. The danger we fall into is to presume that White American culture is not really culture but the norm and that all other cultures must be abandoned for what is "normal" (White American culture). This is a key example of one of the privileges of being White.

In a video documentary on race called *The Color of Fear,* an ethnically diverse group of men gather over a weekend to discuss race in America and to explore the possibilities of racial healing. The ethnic-minority men become frustrated as one of the White men alludes to the idea that all ethnic people should just become Americans if they live in the United States. It is clear that this man defines American culture as White—those things that Whites value and believe in. The situation becomes very tense when the White man simply cannot see his own ethnocentrism. Neither can he believe that the men of color in the room could honestly

---

[3]Lausanne Theology and Education Group, *The Willowbank Report on Gospel and Culture* (Willowbank, Somerset Bridge, Bermuda: Lausanne Committee for World Evangelization, January 6-13, 1978).

be experiencing so much pain over issues of race and ethnicity. In his mind their experiences with racism and White American culture just could not be that bad.

After he explores the possibility that it *is* that bad, he breaks down and is finally able to listen to the concerns of the other men and the struggles they have with White American culture.

EXTERNAL CULTURE
MUSIC, DANCE, FOOD, ART, ETC.
(Visible, easy to change)

INTERNAL CULTURE
VALUES, BELIEFS, THOUGHT, PATTERNS, PERCEPTION
(Not visible, difficult to change)

Figure 6. The cultural iceberg, based on Gary R. Weaver's "Understanding and Coping with Cross-Cultural Adjustment Stress," in *Cross-Cultural Orientation: New Conceptualization and Application*, ed. R. Michael Paige (Lanham, Md.: University Press of America, 1986), pp. 134-46.

Eric H. F. Law compares culture to two parts of an iceberg: external culture and internal culture. *External culture* is a small part of the iceberg, the part we can see above the water. It includes those things we see and hear, like music, art, food and dance. These are the things Law says can be learned and also changed.

The larger *internal culture* is the instinctual part we cannot see but that guides what we think and perceive and how we act. As in the *Willowbank Report*, it includes values, beliefs and cultural myths. We cannot see these things, and therefore they are difficult to change. We understand the world based on these unconscious values and thought patterns. We also interact with our world instinctively in relation to these beliefs and values.[4] Figure 6 helps to picture the external and internal parts of culture.

In the end we cannot stop ourselves from functioning as cultural beings. As we interact with one another and with God, all of these external and internal cultural patterns are present whether we want to admit it or not.

Law points out the relational benefits of having an awareness of the internal, instinctual part of our culture: "The more we learn about our internal culture, the more we are aware of how our cultural values and thought patterns differ from others'. Knowing this difference will help us make self-adjustments in order to live peacefully with people from other cultures."[5]

But it is particularly difficult to identify the internal values that motivate and guide our actions, for they are hidden deep within us. As I tried to distinguish some of my internal cultural values, I struggled until I came across a list composed by Carmen Ross. At the risk of overgeneralizing American and Puerto Rican internal cultural values, I present this list as table 1 because some of the values listed were very enlightening to me. I realized that submissiveness and deference to others, for example, had been ingrained in me as a child. This helped me understand why I had almost always been willing to let others have their way even when I knew I was right on an issue. I still tend to let others have their

---

[4]Eric H. F. Law, *The Wolf Shall Dwell with the Lamb: A Spirituality for Leadership in a Multicultural Community* (St. Louis: Chalice Press, 1993), p. 5.
[5]Ibid., p. 9.

Table 1. Comparison of American and Puerto Rican Value Systems (adapted from Carmen Ross)

American	Puerto Rican
1. Human beings have control over the universe and their own destiny.	1. Universe is controlled by external forces, and so is human destiny (fatalism).
2. Optimistic outlook on life; humankind and its conditions are improvable.	2. Pessimistic outlook on life; human beings must resign themselves to adversity.
3. The nuclear family concept, independence and self-reliance.	3. The extended family and the obligation to each other.
4. Greater equality of the sexes, more freedom, independence and self-reliance among women.	4. Male superiority (machismo), protection and shelter of women.
5. Male and female roles are more interchangeable than a decade ago.	5. Male and female roles are separated at an early age and rigidly delineated.
6. Respect for human achievements and material possessions.	6. Belief in the innate dignity and worth of the person; worth is not in one's achievements, material or otherwise (humanistic values).
7. Greater emphasis on materialism, making physical conditions more comfortable.	7. Greater emphasis on spiritual values and self-perfection.
8. Personality development, refinement and deference to others are less valued traits.	8. Personalism and concomitant values of pride, honor and respect.
9. Assertiveness, initiative and action orientation are highly prized traits.	9. Submissiveness, deference to others and passivity are the ultimate "civilized" behavior.
10. Children's upbringing stresses independence and self-reliance.	10. Children's upbringing stresses obedience and respect for parental authority.
11. Friendship patterns are casual, friendly and committed.	11. Friendship patterns are restrictive, involving complete commitment, loyalty and devotion (*compadrazco* system).
12. Future oriented; places a high value on technology and progress.	12. Past oriented, places a high value on tradition.

way, but now I am aware of this internal dynamic, and when it is necessary I am able go against the grain of my culture and stand my ground—
though with feelings of discomfort.

Since living without internal and external culture is impossible, as
followers of Christ we must invite God to reveal all of our cultural values, beliefs and customs so that they can be conformed into his image.
As we understand better the things we do unconsciously and why we
do them, we will be better able to submit our lives to Christ with clarity
and decisiveness.

Ethnicity, then, does not have to compete with our faith but can be
aligned with God's purposes, give us affirmation we need and help us in
our relationships with others.

PARALLEL JOURNEYS

As I reflect on my life, I realize that my ethnic journey and my spiritual
journey have run parallel with each other, often zigzagging across each
other. At certain times these parallel journeys have melded into one single
line. When I learned something from the Scriptures about God, it deep-
ened and enriched my understanding of self and others. When I grew in
my understanding and commitment to live out of a strong ethnic self, my
eyes were opened to understand God and the Scriptures more fully.

I call this the *interactive view* of Christian discipleship, as opposed to
the *singular view,* which abandons or deemphasizes ethnicity, leaving
only an incomplete, generic brand of Christian faith that can actually
hinder the gospel's power. Figure 7 illustrates these two views.

Here is an example of how I have experienced the interactive journeys
of faith and ethnic identity. Several years ago I was distressed about confronting a close friend of my family who was much older than I. Someone had been hurt by his words, and he needed to know the harm he

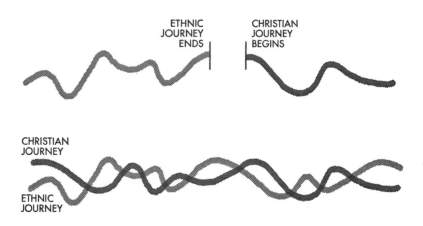

Figure 7. Singular and interactive views of ethnicity and faith

had done. As I struggled with what to do, it became an issue of obedience to God. Was I willing to speak the truth to our friend so he could realize the effects of his actions on others and stop acting irresponsibly?

I am usually pretty quick to obey God when I know what he is calling me to do. In this situation, however, I became immobilized with confusion and fear. In my frustration I turned to God for wisdom. He showed me some cultural barriers that I had never quite put my finger on before. My parents had always ingrained in us respect for our elders. Even to speak to an older person using the familiar word for "you" (*tu* rather than the more formal *usted*) could be taken as an insult.

Once I identified this internal value of honoring and respecting elders, I was able to pray more specifically and obey God by confronting our family friend with respect but also firmness. In the end, he received my rebuke and began to change his actions. Our friendship grew, and my faith soared with renewed trust in God.

LOVE YOURSELF: THE THIRD COMMANDMENT

Even Jesus affirmed a healthy self-love and identity that are not separate from our life of faith and obedience. When asked which was the greatest commandment, Jesus responded, "'Hear, O Israel, the Lord our God, the Lord is one. Love the Lord your God with all your heart and with all your soul and with all your mind and with all your strength.' The second is this: 'Love your neighbor *as yourself*.' There is no commandment greater than these'" (Mark 12:29-31, emphasis added). When reading this passage we often assume Jesus has given just two commands, but he actually gives three: You are to love God. You are to love others. And you are to love yourself. If you have never loved yourself, which includes your ethnic self, your ability to love others will be distorted and incomplete.

What does it mean to love yourself? What is the self? Is it not the sum of all that we are? We are to love our appearance and our intellect. We are to love those distinctive qualities that God has blessed us with. We are to love even the peculiar things about us that endear us to others. I am always amazed that my wife continues to love me despite my idiosyncrasies. In fact, she has said that she loves me *more* because of them, since these are the little things that make me who I am.

Loving ourselves fully must include our ethnicity and culture. Are these not pieces of the self Jesus calls us to love? When Jesus says to love others as we love ourselves, the assumption is that we know instinctively how to love ourselves. Clear self-knowledge prepares us to love others fully, without a demanding spirit or self-protection.

As you grow in your ethnic identity you learn to love yourself, your people, your culture and the culture of others. Our growth in each area of our life does not compete with our commitment to God but becomes another tool God uses to conform us into his image and accomplish his will.

QUESTIONS FOR REFLECTION AND DISCUSSION

1. When was the last time you heard a sermon or message that dealt with ethnicity or culture? Summarize what was mentioned.

2. Think about your church experience. How has your church life affirmed or denied your ethnicity?

3. Make a list of the internal and external cultural values that have shaped or continue to shape your life. Underline the values that were not obvious to you at first.

4. How have your faith and your ethnicity remained separate in your life? How have they influenced one another or merged together?

5. What are some ways an undeveloped ethnic identity can prevent us from fully loving God and our neighbor?

7

❀

RACIAL RECONCILIATION
AL SABOR LATINA (LATINO-STYLE)

*Uncovering our own internal culture will take a lifetime. We
can speed up the process by seeking to encounter others who
are different. In the cultural point of view it is like a fish
being pulled out of the water and discovering for the first time
that the water had been its total life context. A fish out of
the water is not comfortable. Its life is in danger. That is how it
feels sometimes when we are being pulled outside our
cultural water so that we can see what our culture looks like
from the other's point of view. We can feel very threatened and
insecure. Our instinct is to jump back into our cultural water.
Our instinct is to run and hide. But as Christians, we are often
called to go against our instinct.*

ERIC H. F. LAW, *THE WOLF SHALL DWELL WITH THE LAMB*

I have had the opportunity to move within Christian circles where racial
reconciliation, the pursuit of racial and ethnic healing, is considered an
important value and a necessary objective for the church. In many dia-
logues on race I have been the sole Latino voice. These times have been

intimidating as I have attempted to speak out for an incredibly diverse Latino community. However, I have accepted the reality that if I don't speak out, the Latino perspective will be overlooked. I have decided that I must speak out, even at the risk of getting something wrong.

In one race discussion a White participant asked how minorities could promote ethnic identity and still be committed to racial and ethnic reconciliation. "Doesn't this undermine our ability to be united?" he said. At the moment I was too hesitant to respond but as I thought about it later I realized that ethnic identity development and racial reconciliation are two sides of the same coin.

To me it is very simple. As I studied Puerto Rican and Latino history, I became bitter and angry toward the United States and toward Whites in particular. U.S. policies of gunboat diplomacy, the long-term colonization of Puerto Rico, the stealing of Mexican land and ongoing institutional racism against Latinos in America are enough to make anyone feel anger and hatred.

Because hatred is not an option for me as a Christian, I have chosen the route of dialogue with Whites and others to help me deal with the deep pain and sadness of racism and social injustice. Without a doubt it has been a strong ethnic identity—that has involved an understanding of the present needs of Latinos and an honest view of our nation's racial history—that has prepared me to express my pain and seek peace with my White brothers and sisters.

This chapter will briefly outline racial reconciliation. It will also delineate two important steps that have helped me to enter into discussions about race. First, we Latinos must understand the complexities of race amongst ourselves because ignorance has sometimes kept us from entering into the dialogue. And second, Latinos have certain strengths that can strike a death blow at our passivity and inspire us to speak out with conviction, truthfulness and love. We must know what those strengths are so we can faithfully live them out in the context of racial reconciliation.

STEPS TO AUTHENTIC RACIAL RECONCILIATION

An outline I have found very helpful in understanding what racial reconciliation should look like comes from Randy Woodley's book entitled *Living in Color: Embracing God's Passion for Diversity*. Just recently I had the opportunity to get to know Randy and his family as we traveled with a group of InterVarsity campus ministers. Randy was our instructor in helping us understand Native American history as an important part of American history. A Cherokee Indian, Randy has inspired me with his vision of what the church in America could be if we took reconciliation seriously and made room for authentic cultural diversity that gives freedom to every culture to worship God in its own context. To bring out biblical healing, seven crucial steps are necessary based on Randy's chapter titled "Getting Beyond Getting Along."[1] The steps are:

1. *Sincere, devout listening.* We must listen to the pain, the guilt, the shame and oppression. Speaking should occur only when necessary.

   a. "He who answers before listening—that is his folly and his shame" (Proverbs 18:13).

   b. "Let the wise listen and add to their learning" (Proverbs 1:5).

2. *Confession of the wrong done.* "We can never substitute forgiveness from each other for God's forgiveness unless He is part and parcel of the equation."[2] Healing has divine and human components that we cannot overlook.

---

[1]Randy Woodley, *Living in Color: Embracing God's Passion for Diversity* (Grand Rapids: Baker, 2001), pp. 162-80.
[2]Ibid., p. 166.

a. "Confess your sins one to each other and pray for each other so that you may be healed" (James 5:16).

b. "If you are offering your gift at the altar and there remember that your brother has something against you, leave your gift there in front of the altar. First go and be reconciled to your brother; then come and offer your gift" (Matthew 5:23-24).

3. *Repentance.* It is a turning away from sin that leads to change in what we say and how we live. *Identificational repentance* has to do with identifying with the injustices perpetrated by our race or culture upon another race or culture.

a. "Produce fruit in keeping with repentance" (Matthew 3:8).

b. "I confess the sins we Israelites, including myself and my father's house, have committed against you. We have acted very wickedly toward you. We have not obeyed the commands, decrees and laws you gave your servant Moses" (Nehemiah 1:6-7).

4. *Forgiveness of the offense.* Forgiveness is extended after sincere confession of sin is made.

a. "Forgive us our debts, as we also have forgiven our debtors. . . . For if you forgive men when they sin against you, your heavenly Father will also forgive you. But if you do not forgive men their sins, your Father will not forgive your sins" (Matthew 6:12, 14-15).

b. "Love your enemies, do good to those who hate you, bless those who curse you, pray for those who mistreat you" (Luke 6:27-28).

c. "Do not repay anyone evil for evil. Be careful to do what is right in the eyes of everybody. If it is possible, as far as it depends on you, live at peace with everyone" (Romans 12:17-18).

5. *Restitution to the appropriate person.* With true repentance must come the commitment to consider the loss or damage done to the injured party. Restitution fuels the process of wholeness and healing. It leaves a visible indication that the injustice has been resolved and clears those who have done the offense of any lasting feelings of guilt. The beneficiaries of an injustice should make restitution with those in the "closest line of contact" who have suffered wrong.

   a. "'Tell the people that men and women alike are to ask their neighbors for articles of silver and gold.' (The Lord made the Egyptians favorably disposed toward the people)" (Exodus 11:2-3).

   b. "The Lord said to Moses: 'If anyone sins and is unfaithful to the Lord by deceiving his neighbor about something entrusted to him or left in his care or stolen, or if he cheats him, or if he finds lost property and lies about it, or if he swears falsely, or if he commits any such sin that people may do—when he thus sins and becomes guilty, he must return what he has stolen or taken by extortion, or what was entrusted to him, or the lost property he found, or whatever it was he swore falsely about. He must make restitutions in full, add a fifth of the value to it and give it all to the owner on the day he presents his guilt offering'" (Leviticus 6:1-5).

   c. "When a man or woman wrongs another in any way and so is unfaithful to the Lord, that person is guilty and must confess the sin he has committed. He must make full restitutions for his wrong, add one fifth to it and give it all to the person he has wronged. But if that person has no close relative to whom restitution can be made for the wrong, the restitution belongs to the Lord and must be given to the priest, along with the ram with which atonement is made for him" (Numbers 5:5-8).

6. *Healing land that has been defiled.* "God has a vested interest in our healing the land. . . . As human beings we have cursed the land, and we are the ones who must pronounce its redemption in Christ."[3]

   a. "When I shut up the heavens so that there is no rain, or command locust to devour the land or send a plague among my people, if my people, who are called by my name, will humble themselves and pray and seek my face and turn from their wicked ways, then will I hear from heaven and will forgive their sin and will heal their land" (2 Chronicles 7:13-14).

   b. "I looked for a man among them who would build up the wall and stand before me in the gap on behalf of the land so I would not have to destroy it, but I found none" (Ezekiel 22:30).

   c. "How long will the land lie parched and the grass in every field be withered? Because those who live in it are wicked . . . it will be made a wasteland, parched and desolate before me; the whole land will be laid waste because there is no one who cares" (Jeremiah 12: 4, 11).

7. *Renewed relationships between the parties involved.*

   a. "His purpose was to create in himself one new man out of the two, thus making peace, and in this one body to reconcile both of them to God through the cross, by which he put to death their hostility" (Ephesians 2: 15b-16).

   b. "Get rid of all bitterness, rage and anger, brawling and slander, along with every form of malice. Be kind and compassionate to one another, forgiving each other, just as in Christ God forgave you" (Ephesians 4:31-32).

---

[3]Ibid., p. 176.

Before we can pursue racial reconciliation it is necessary to understand what true reconciliation looks like. In our desire to move on with our life we often skip over one of the steps with devastating results because the falsehood of it is eventually exposed. I have met many Christians who want to skip over the part that has to do with restitution because it is so tricky and because it will mean some loss of resources to us. Greed is the great sin of America. It would follow then that this step of restitution is the hardest for us. Yet I believe it is the step that eventually will bring tangible and lasting healing to our nation.

THE DYNAMICS OF RACE: A PUERTO RICAN VIEW

I had the privilege of growing up with a mother and father who modeled love and perseverance and four siblings who valued my achievements. They were patient with me even when I made poor decisions or messed up. I was extremely clumsy as a kid. I don't want to remember how many rugs I ruined with spilled coffee or how many lamps I broke with a misplaced elbow at just the wrong moment. I used to have plenty of wrong moments. In fact, they used to call me—and sometimes still do—*nunca falla,* which means "never fails." In other words, "He never fails to break something." I still don't believe them when they try to convince me how clumsy I was. And they can't believe I'm still in denial about the whole thing. Without a doubt, we enjoy being together as a family even in our many faults and differences.

Take our difference in skin tone for example. My brother, Edwin, is quite dark, while my younger sister Sandra is very light skinned and burns easily in the sun. My youngest sister, Milagro, who is the prettiest of us all, has an olive skin tone that makes her quite striking. My sister Marilyn and I have a similar light olive complexion. As a family we did not seem to fit into either Black or White categories of race. We simply saw ourselves as non-White, based on our Puerto Rican ethnicity. This made it interesting for some of our Black and White friends, who really didn't know where we fit in regarding their Black-White racial paradigm of the world.

One of my regrets growing up, however, was using our skin tones against each other. Whenever we became angry at my brother Edwin, for example, we would use his dark skin against him and call him "nigger" to hurt him. We had bought into and were affected by racism even as children. It had permeated into our relationships and leaked out at the most volatile moments. Of course, my brother was very good at defending himself and would come back at us with some name he knew would hurt us.

In an earlier chapter I spoke about *mestizaje* as an important paradigm to understand the Latino ethnic journey in the Americas. Parallel to *mestizaje* is *mulatez*, the mixture of African and Spanish blood. In Puerto Rico, where a large percentage of the indigenous Taino Indians were quickly killed off once Europeans began arriving, a mixture of Blacks and Whites became the dominant people group. Puerto Ricans belong to both groups, yet we are neither Black nor White. In purely racial terms we can be categorized in both groups, but ethnically we belong to neither group.

In Puerto Rico cultural identification supersedes racial identification. Clara E. Rodriguez, professor of sociology at Fordham College at Lincoln Center in New York City and editor of a book entitled *Historical Perspectives on Puerto Rican Survival in the United States*, writes,

> In Puerto Rico racial identification is subordinate to cultural identification, while in the U.S. racial identification, to a large extent, determines cultural identification. Thus when asked that divisive question, "What are you?" Puerto Ricans of all colors and ancestry

answer, "Puerto Rican." . . . This is not to say that Puerto Ricans feel no racial identification, but rather that cultural identification supersedes it.[4]

Racial classification is not simply based on biological descent but on a combination of physical appearance and social class. Rodriguez points out that if you are dark skinned but from a higher social class, you are classified at a higher level than a dark-skinned person of a lower social class. Class, skin color, facial features and hair type all factor into racial classification. There are five main racial categories used in Puerto Rico.

1. *Blanco:* what we would consider White in the United States. My sister Sandra would fit this category.

2. *Indio:* similar to our concept of East Indian, people with dark skin and straight hair.

3. *Moreno:* dark skinned. My brother Edwin would fit into this category.

4. *Negro* (pronounced neg'-row): Blacks. *Negro* or *negra* is also used as a term of affection for anyone of any racial type.

5. *Trigueño* (tree-gen'-yo, with a hard *g*): equivalent to brunette in the United States, or can even be used for a *negro* with a high social status. This term clearly shows the relationship between class and race in Puerto Rico.

Because I grew up with this Puerto Rican paradigm of race, it has been difficult for me to know where to enter into the dialogue of race in the United States. For the most part it has not made sense to me, and for a time I chose to ignore or avoid the tough race issues. Rodriguez helps to explain this:

---

[4]Clara E. Rodriguez, "Puerto Ricans: Between Black and White" in *Historical Perspectives on Puerto Rican Survival in the United States,* ed. Clara E. Rodriguez (Princeton, N.J.: Markus Wiener, 1996), p. 26.

There are only two options open in biracial New York—to be white or black. These options negate the cultural existence of Puerto Ricans and ignore their insistence on being treated, irrespective of race, as a culturally intact group. Thus, U.S. racial attitudes necessarily make Puerto Ricans either white or black, attitudes and culture make them neither white nor black, and our own resistance and struggle for survival place us between whites and blacks. This struggle for survival has not left Puerto Ricans unaffected. On the contrary, this in-between position has affected individual perceptions as well as group identity. Historically, Puerto Ricans arriving in New York have found themselves in a situation of perceptual incongruence—that is, they saw themselves differently than they were seen.[5]

Puerto Ricans, a culturally homogenous, racially integrated group, do not want to be racially divided and stripped of their Puerto Rican identity just to fit in. Puerto Ricans have straddled the Black-White categorizations for many years, preferring to be in the category of "non-White." Rodriguez asks,

What does the term "non-white" mean? Is this a racial term? Non-white is to New York Puerto Ricans what Puerto Ricans and blacks are; "white" is what Puerto Ricans and blacks are not. This increasingly common definition of Puerto Ricans as "non-white" can also be seen as an evolution of racial perceptions and classifications engendered in Puerto Rico. For the predominance of cultural over racial considerations is evident in the development of this new "racial" term, which embraces all colors and types of Puerto Ricans.[6]

[5]Ibid., p. 32.
[6]Ibid., p. 33.

As you can see, here again the Latino experience in this country is multilayered and complicated. It has taken many of us a lifetime to figure out where we stand. It has also made us reluctant to address issues of race, not only because we are dealing with an entirely different view of race in this country but also because race is not discussed in the same way among Latinos. I do not remember any constructive conversations on race in my Latino community during my growing-up years.

Yet I believe it is crucial for us to speak strongly in representing Latinos in settings where race is discussed openly. What then are some helpful ways we can enter into the race dialogue?

OUR OWN STRUGGLES WITH RACE

To have anything to offer in the race dialogue, we must come to terms with our own prejudices and the contradictions that are prevalent in our own communities yet are rarely addressed. Ilan Stavans, author of *The Hispanic Condition: Reflections on Culture and Identity in America*, states in his book that the multiplicity of race is taboo among Latinos and is not openly discussed:

> From bronze-skinned to mulatto, from snow white to indio, ours are wide-ranging colors—but a long-standing, rampant racism running through our blood remains unanalyzed. Yes, *racismo*. Society is silent when the word is uttered. Nobody takes responsibility. Nobody listens. In the United States, a nation obsessed with racial and cultural wars, we Latinos are ambiguous, suspicious, and uncomfortable.[7]

As I mentioned earlier, this racism has been evident in my own family. Eighteen years ago I visited a close relative whom I respected and cher-

---

[7]Ilan Stavans, *The Hispanic Condition: Reflections on Culture and Identity in America* (New York: HarperCollins Publishers, 1995), pp. 103-4.

ished. As I sat with her on her front porch, taking in a warm summer breeze and enjoying the fragrance of her roses, I confided that I was seriously thinking of marrying my girlfriend Maritza, an Afro-Cuban woman. She looked away from me and said that it would be unfortunate if I did because my children would feel less loved than my cousin's children when they came to visit her.

I was confused at first. *Less loved? What is she saying? How could my children feel badly about the color of their skin unless someone made them feel that way by treating them badly?* I soon realized that she was telling me, even though she would not have admitted it, that she would treat my children with less love, affection and care because of their darker skin color.

I left her home with pain in my heart, wondering if I could ever recover from her soft-spoken yet crushing remarks.

My friend Esteban recalls similar language whenever a new child was born in his family. If the baby was light skinned, there was jubilant admiration. *"Ay, pero qué blanquito salió ese nene. Qué chulo."* (My, this baby turned out so white. How adorable!) But if the baby happened to be dark, family members would say: *"Qué oscuro es este nene. Pero no tiene que ver, está lindo."* (This baby is so dark. But no matter, he is still cute.)

We Latinos must acknowledge our own prejudices and self-hatred. In doing so we get in touch with the pain of racism and the contradictions we have within ourselves. Until we do that, we will not experience the healing that is needed in order to be reconcilers with non-Latinos.

Much Latino racism, as I said earlier, is an outgrowth of the self-hatred that stems from dominant-subdominate experiences in any society. But it does not matter where it comes from. What should matter is that we become reconciled with ourselves. As we reconcile with ourselves as

Latinos, we are in a better place to achieve reconciliation with other racial and ethnic groups with integrity.

It has been helpful for me to begin acknowledging my own prejudices against and resentments of other Latino groups. I have had to admit that I have held certain prejudices against White Cubans. I was convinced that all the White Cubans I met thought they were better than me because I am Puerto Rican, or my wife because she is Afro-Cuban. My initial interactions with them were always marked by self-protectiveness, hesitancy to be open for fear of being hurt by their subtle or not-so-subtle sense of superiority. I was often surprised when it turned out that the White Cuban was actually *simpático* (pleasant, humble) and *amable* (personable). It finally dawned on me that I had a prejudice that I needed to deal with and surrender to God.

Even as I write these words it is difficult to admit that I have held biases against other Latinos. I know how painful it is to be the recipient of prejudice, and yet I was doing the very thing I despised to my own Latino brothers and sisters.

We must be willing to acknowledge how we have hurt each other within our own Latino communities through our prejudices and stereotypes. We must be willing to confess these before God and one another and begin to dismantle these views in ourselves and our community actively, by challenging negative remarks made about each other and by setting a new standard, telling new stories that go against the grain of longstanding negative stereotypes of each other and by openly discussing race issues with each other.

SEEK CONSENSUS, SPEAK WITH ONE VOICE

As we address racial issues amongst ourselves and begin to enter into race dialogue with non-Latinos, it is imperative that we understand how much we Latinos have to offer. If we are not convinced of this, it will be very easy to hold back and not get involved.

Several years ago a group of campus ministers met for a conference in which racial reconciliation was the main theme. We were all tense as we launched into difficult large-group discussions on issues of diversity. On several occasions we broke into smaller ethnic-specific groups to process how the conversation was affecting us.

The next day as we were invited to summarize our conversations, several from the Latino delegation felt a tremendous sense of courage and willingness to speak honestly. They had the courage to speak for all of us in saying, for example, that we were frustrated with the fact that most of the race dialogue was centered around Black-White tensions and little attention was being given to Latinos. As the fastest-growing minority in the United States, we said, we were all seeing the landscape changing quickly, yet we as Christians were not adapting to it in our dialogue. We also clarified that we were uncomfortable with the conference's overall method for dealing with race issues: spending most of our time in the larger group often did not give us enough time to process what we were hearing and hammer out together what our formal response should be.

But somehow, because we were speaking for the entire Latino group after reaching agreement on these issues, we could speak strongly and with confidence. We discovered that we were cautious about speaking generally for the entire Latino community without consensus, for fear we might reflect our views more than the community's.

If God has called you to enter into the race dialogue, the assurance that you speak on behalf of other Latinos will fill you with the courage you need. This will offset the corrosive power of self-doubt during painful discussions of power, racism, justice and reconciliation. However, as often as you are able, it will be important to spend time with other Latinos, to process information and decide together how to respond to issues debated in a large group setting.

RECOGNIZING OUR PARTICULAR GIFTING

Because of our racial diversity and the marginalization Latinos have experienced, we can actually make important contributions in bringing racial healing to our nation. Below is a list of some values that are present in the Latino community and can be helpful in this process of racial and ethnic healing. Those of us who take our Christian faith seriously must be committed to the health of our relationships with our White, Black, Asian and Native American sisters and brothers.

We are relational and value harmony. We are a very relational people and care passionately about family, our country, our friendships and our God. We must learn to funnel this passion into deep concern for racial and ethnic reconciliation so that we are moved to speak and act despite our hesitations.

We also value harmony in relationships. I have seen Latinos go to extremes to sustain harmony in good and bad ways. We will intervene as moderator between two friends in conflict because we cannot stand to see them live in tension with one another. We will open up our pocketbooks to help a close friend or family member in an emergency no matter what negative long-term effects this might have on our own immediate family. Unfortunately, at times we will also practice avoidance and endure relational dissonance for years in order to retain at least the appearance of harmony. While this is an issue we must continue to grow in, our commitment to harmony is an important value God can redeem in us if we can move beyond family relationships and apply it to broader issues amongst ethnic and racial groups. We could become shalom-makers (peacemakers), working behind the scenes to bring harmony in difficult situations that we might otherwise want to avoid.

As I have studied this biblical concept of shalom it has brought me hope because it is a biblical concept that addresses the entire needs of a community. It is impossible for example to have shalom if even one person does not have what she needs to live. Shalom is a state where harmony is reached because everyone's basic needs for community and sustenance are met. I am grateful for an important book I read recently by Walter Brueggemann called *Peace* that gave me a clear understanding of harmony through shalom. He writes:

> It is well-being of a material, physical, historical kind, not idyllic "pie in the sky," but "salvation" in the midst of trees and crops and enemies—in the very places where people always have to cope with anxiety, to struggle for survival, and to deal with temptation. It is well-being of a very personal kind—the address in Leviticus 26 is to a single person, but it is also deliberately corporate. If there is to be well-being, it will not be just for isolated, insulated individuals: it is, rather, security and prosperity granted to a whole community—young and old, rich and poor, powerful and dependent. Always we are all in it together. Together we stand before God's blessings and together we receive the gift of life, if we receive it at all. Shalom comes only to the inclusive, embracing community that excludes none.[8]

Therefore, as Latinos we must be concerned for harmony not only within our own families but we must extend this to include others we may perceive as being on the outside of our community and family. We

---

[8] Walter Brueggemann, *Peace* (St. Louis: Chalice Press, 2001), p. 15.

must transfer this strong harmony ethic to others who are non-Latinos in need of the strength of community we bring with us so that together as Brueggemann mentions we might receive the blessings of God as an inclusive and embracing diverse people.

We are multiracial. Because of our history, Latinos stand on many sides of the race divisions. As a White Latino, I am unhappy when fellow Latinos assume I am White and remain distant. I want to make it clear, "I am not White!" so they will take me in as a brother. I have also been the recipient of White privilege, when a White person trusts me because they think I am White. But I have also experienced the pain of racism when I am treated with suspicion with my dark hair, goatee and tan complexion in a summertime crowd of blond-haired, blue-eyed people.

Standing between two worlds culturally, linguistically and often racially affords me the ability to relate to parties on different ends of the race issue. What I must learn to do is move from empathy to action that leads to dialogue, understanding and restoration.

We are hospitable. Hospitality is a very important feature of Latino culture. If we happened to have unexpected guests for dinner when I was a child, I would eat much less food so that our guests could share the meal with us. In Puerto Rican culture it is considered an honor if a friend comes by to see you without calling you. It means they care enough about you to drop by and honor you with their presence. I recall my parents going out of their way to welcome and accommodate the unexpected guests. Only occasionally when they were feeling an extraordinary amount of fatigue would they mutter under their breath.

With the help of God this ability to welcome can be developed beyond friend-and-family hospitality to the welcoming of strangers. In painful situations of racial and ethnic difficulty, hospitality and welcome can serve as release valves to alleviate tension and bring hope. I have been to multiethnic conferences where Latinos have offered gifts of music to bless Whites struggling to understand White privilege and the ugly history of racism in the United States. In the midst of the voices and the strumming, tears were shed in appreciation for our gentle spirit of hospitality.

We are many. The Latino population is growing larger and larger. One estimate places us at around forty million strong in the United States, with those who are undocumented and the over three million Puerto Ricans who live on the island of Puerto Rico included. Given the continuing growth of the Latino population, it is obvious that we must enter into constructive dialogue with others on issues of race and ethnicity. For example, the dominant culture in America in the past has done an exceptional job of pitting ethnic groups against each other, especially when resources have been scarce. As the Latino population grows we must be careful that the media not present us as a threat to the African American community. After all, the Black community in many ways has paved the way for other ethnic groups to have greater civil rights and freedoms. Instead, as Latinos we must realize that we are fighting the same battles as other ethnic groups in affordable housing, educational inequities and business opportunities. It will only be through open and honest dialogue that unity and shalom will come to all our ethnic and racial communities in need. As Latinos we need to be the ones who start leading in these areas instead of waiting for others to lead justly.

We understand racism and marginalization. As a community we understand what it feels like to experience racism, oppression and injustice. We can therefore speak to the issues with empathy and wisdom. We are not a third party standing in between Blacks and Whites with nothing to gain or lose; rather, we are able to enter into the dialogue and face the challenges because racist practices affect our lives as well. This should serve as a powerful incentive for us to care about what is happening in our country, our communities and our places of employment in regard to race and ethnicity.

We can celebrate even in the midst of pain. Racial division and injustice are no laughing matter. However, there are times when laughter and celebration are the very thing that is needed to bring people together and open them up to looking at issues in a different light. Over the years my wife and I have had heated discussions over finances, ministry and child-rearing. What has rescued us from becoming mired in cynicism, frustration and bitterness has been our ability to laugh at ourselves. Laughing has helped us to lighten up and approach the situation more objectively and as partners committed to finding a solution together.

Being able to celebrate life in the midst of pain means that we are not allowing our problems to overwhelm our entire lives. We remind ourselves that we are brothers and sisters on a journey of life that is bigger than our temporary or longstanding sufferings. If we Latinos could take this gift into racially charged situations, we could help usher in laughter, levity and joy that could break the stronghold of mistrust.

In conclusion, I have touched on two key issues that are pivotal in motivating Latinos to enter into discussions about race: our need to understand the complexities of race using a Puerto Rican perspective and the tangible strengths we bring to racial reconciliation. As we understand how we as Latinos view race we must take steps to dismantle racism amongst ourselves so that God might release the full potential of our gifts as a community to our American neighbors of all ethnicities and races. Our intention as followers of Christ should never be about "us trying to get ours" but about a view of wholeness in "which persons are bound not only to God but to one another in a caring, sharing, rejoicing community with none to make them afraid."[9] Finally, we must remember—and it is hard to do when racial injustice is involved—that none of this would be possible without a loving God who has already gone ahead of us and has made our unity with him and each other possible. It is through the supreme but joyful sacrifice of the life, death and resurrection of his Son, Jesus Christ, that we can even begin to speak about genuine and lasting reconciliation. With him it is hard but possible. Without our God's help it is utterly futile. "For [Jesus] is our peace; in his flesh he has made both groups into one and has broken down the dividing wall, that is, the hostility between us" (Ephesians 2:14 NRSV).

QUESTIONS FOR REFLECTION AND DISCUSSION

1. What positive or negative experiences have you had as you have interacted with other Latinos regarding issues of race and ethnicity within your own Latino community?

2. How do you understand the connection between ethnic identity formation and pursuing racial reconciliation? How can they strengthen or weaken each other?

3. What are some of the prejudices Latinos have against other Latinos? What stereotypes and prejudices did your family have regarding other Latinos?

4. Using a number between 1 and 10, assess your willingness and commitment to enter into difficult race and ethnicity conversations with non-Latinos. Why would you rate yourself in this way?

5. Based on some of the strengths mentioned that Latinos can bring to the reconciliation table, do you see some of these strengths present in

---

[9]Ibid.

your own life? In your family? In your community?

6. Are there other strengths the Latino community brings to racial reconciliation? How can these help us move forward?

7. Spend some time in prayer. Invite God to help us progress in racial and ethnic healing amongst ourselves as Latinos and with non-Latino communities. Pray for specific areas of need.

8

※

BICULTURALISM AND MINISTRY
SERVING OTHERS WELL

If you have any encouragement from being united with Christ,
if any comfort from his love, if any fellowship with the Spirit,
if any tenderness and compassion, then make my joy complete
by being like-minded, having the same love, being one in
spirit and purpose. Do nothing out of selfish ambition or vain
conceit, but in humility consider others better than yourselves.
Each of you should look not only to your own interests, but
also to the interests of others.
Your attitude should be the same as that of Christ Jesus.

PHILIPPIANS 2:1-5

The United States is quickly becoming more and more multiracial. Every year an increasing number of major newsmagazines highlight this fact and point us to what is in store for the United States in the next two or three decades. However, every single article I have read ignores the fact that Latinos are centuries ahead of the United States when it comes to race mixing as I have pointed out in earlier chapters. Since the fabric of our very existence as Latinos is multiracial (*mestizaje*), I am convinced

God is placing us in a strategic position to use our strengths to be a blessing to this nation. This chapter examines one particular strength many Latinos have that comes out of being multiracial and often multicultural: biculturalism. I want to tell some stories of how Latinos have stepped out and made a difference for others through their biculturalism and what we can learn from them.

CULTURAL INTERPRETERS

Biculturalism is the capability to have two worlds in one's head and live in both of these worlds with some degree of proficiency. A bicultural person can value both worlds yet see the negatives and the positives of both simultaneously. Biculturalism is also the ability to interpret these different worlds or cultures to those who cannot fully understand or appreciate them.

In college a Latino friend of mine and a White friend were at odds regarding a decision that had to be made. As they argued, it was clear to me that it had to do with a difference in cultural values. I thought, *They are completely missing each other's point of view. How can they not see it that this has everything to do with underlying cultural values?* So I began serving as a cultural interpreter, filling in information and analysis that each of them had been missing and helping them to overcome their communication meltdown.

Conflicts like these are opportunities for a Latino to serve as a bridge person who can bring clarity and peace in the midst of confusion and frustration. I have learned not to become bitter and resentful of these challenging situations but to utilize my biculturalism as a means to step in and meet a need. Standing in the middle as a bicultural person is a place of ministry where stereotypes are broken and reconciliation can begin. Those of us who are bridge people often get trampled on and

116

hurt. We are in the line of fire. Yet I have also experienced great joy in helping people move back and forth as they learn to value one another and one another's cultures.

Virgilio Elizondo believes that it will be through Mexican Americans that the bridges of communication and understanding will be built between "the two Americas"—that is the United States of *America* and Latin *America.*

> They are two totally different worlds. Each one has its own values, meanings, and symbols. It is not a question of which is better or which is worse. Both are rich in many ways and poor in many ways.
>
> The Mexican-American stands in the midst of both worlds and what in effect appears as an unfinished identity can be the basis for personal understanding and appreciation of two identities. It is through the Mexican-American that the two Americas will meet, know, and love each other.[1]

EMPATHY AND COMPASSION

Biculturalism helps us serve others well because it can instill in us compassion for and empathy with others in need. When I was a campus minister at Hunter College in the early 1990s, one of my students served in a short-term missions trip to Romania. This student was the only Latina in the group; she had never participated in a missions project before and had many doubts about whether she had anything to offer. "I know so little about Romania. The only ministry experience I have is in my small Spanish Pentecostal church in the Bronx. Seriously, Orlando, you gotta get me outta this. I don't even know why I said I would do this mis-

---

[1]Virgilio P. Elizondo, *Galilean Journey: The Mexican American Promise* (Maryknoll, N.Y.: Orbis, 1983), p. 103.

sions trip in the first place. I barely know enough English or Spanish; how am I ever going to learn enough Romanian to make a difference?"

This student had had a very difficult upbringing. After her parents divorced when she was young, her mother was left to raise her and two other children. They had lived in poverty for many years, including suffering through rat infestations, the welfare system, few educational options and many other kinds of urban degradation.

When she arrived in Romania, one of the first things she noticed was that many of the Romanian students were dealing with poverty that was similar to her own experience in the Bronx. It didn't take very long for these students to connect with her on a deep level. They detected in her a level of empathy and compassion that none of the White American students had. This opened up many opportunities for her to build friendship and demonstrate Christian love.

Even after the missions trip my student was able to maintain contact with her new friends through letter writing. God had used her marginalized experience as a Latina to build empathy in her and opportunities to minister to others.

Latinos have much to offer despite the difficult challenges of racism, poverty and marginalization. God desires to raise up many more Latinos, like my student, who are willing to go forward knowing that their weakness can become a great asset in the hands of a creative and compassionate God.

A BLESSING TO BOTH CULTURES

One of my best experiences at Hunter College was getting to know Luis Alvarez, a Dominican American student who was intelligent academically and gifted in ministry. Luis was wise and balanced enough to use his gifts to bless both InterVarsity's ministry and his own church in Spanish Harlem. His biculturalism placed him in a position to receive from one culture and give to the other, and vice versa. Before joining Inter-Varsity, Luis was already a strong leader in his church and had been involved in youth group ministry. These gifts of leadership blessed the ministry of InterVarsity. At Hunter, Luis proved quite gifted in leading small groups. The church he attended in Spanish Harlem did not have a history of small group ministry. What Luis learned through InterVarsity he was able to bring back and incorporate slowly into the church.

Luis's willingness to step forward and actively engage both worlds helped to move him beyond *bendito*—a Spanish saying equivalent to "O woe is me!"—to the biblical truth that anything can be accomplished through Jesus Christ who is our strength. I have stayed in contact with Luis over the years, and I am still amazed at how he has continued to help his church move toward new initiatives that address the core needs of the Latino community.

OPPORTUNITIES IN MISSIONS

Another student who discovered her ethnicity to be a gift for ministry was Rosa DeLeon. Rosa decided to take part in a global missions project in a North African Islamic country. When she arrived, she realized she looked very much like the people she had come to minister to. The very fact that her appearance was similar to theirs gave her an ability to build trust quickly, but it was her interpersonal skills as a bicultural Latina that made the real difference. She was able to get through some very touchy situations and build trust. On one occasion one of the other students on her team wrote some very personal things in her journal about her desire to see her host family become Christians. The journal was found and read by the family and caused quite a stir about the ulterior motives of all those in the project. Rosa managed to navigate through all of the con-

119

troversy and still have a fruitful experience with the entire host family.

On several occasions she was even permitted to enter mosques and other places where only Muslims were normally allowed to enter. Her relational, bicultural strengths and olive skin became great assets to her that summer and for many other summers in North Africa. Her host family took her in as a daughter, and Rosa built close relationships with several family members.

Her experience was so positive that she returned to North Africa many times, directing several missions projects herself. She has maintained contact with her host family and has been able to share the love of Christ with them on many occasions.

Latinos embody a mixture of races and ethnicities that can work to our advantage in missions, especially as resentment against White Americans continues to grow throughout the Arab world. Our bicultural skills, if we continue to understand and develop them, will allow us to go further in crosscultural relationships overseas and here in the United States.

BICULTURALISM DEMANDS COURAGE AND WISDOM

Several years ago the director of Baseball Chapel called me and asked if I would be open to serving as the chaplain for the New York Mets. I met with the outgoing Mets chaplain and even got to lead a chapel service with players like Robin Ventura in attendance. This was the year the Mets played the Yankees in the 2000 World Series. The director responsible for hiring new chaplains pointed out that there were growing numbers of Spanish-speaking Latinos in professional baseball who had no one to minister to them in their language. He was committed to hiring more Latino chaplains who were bicultural and could serve both Latinos and non-Latinos. Although I reluctantly turned down the job (I was kicking myself after the Mets made it to the World Series against the Yankees), the experience of simply being offered the job helped me to feel highly respected and sought after. It confirmed I was in the right job as the director of LaFe, but it also affirmed that my life experiences, ministry training and my ethnic identity were valued beyond my present position.

Friends and professors have similarly helped me realize that opportunities will come my way because of my gifts and because of the growing number of Latinos in this country who need to be served by our predominantly White churches. Latinos who can function in both majority culture and Latino culture will have the greatest opportunities for work and service. Being bicultural is a tremendous asset, not a liability, as it seemed in my early childhood.

The challenges for those who are bicultural will not come from a lack of opportunities for work and ministry. Opportunities and requests will only increase for gifted bicultural, bilingual Latinos. Rather, the challenges will involve wisely choosing which opportunities to accept and which to turn down. I have seen gifted Latinos overextend themselves with church, graduate school, marriage, children and two or three jobs simply because opportunities kept presenting themselves. I am grateful to Pastor Bill Sweeting, a friend and former supervisor, who drilled in my head at an early stage in my ministry training that "if you say yes to one thing, you are actually saying no to something else that may be attractive and appealing to you later." It has been a wise rule of life for me that has kept me from irresponsibility and massive burnout.

It is vital to learn how to make good decisions based on your gift mix, your time constraints and God's call in your life. If you do not make wise decisions, you will be prey to emotional, spiritual and physical exhaustion, marital instability and resentment from your family and friends.

BICULTURALISM PREPARES US FOR MULTICULTURALISM

What is most exciting about living in America is our diversity. I have
been highlighting the value of being bicultural and the many doors for
service it can open up for us. The greatest asset of biculturalism is that it
can be the precursor of true multiethnicity.

Being a *multicultural* person is having an ability to interact with people from many different cultures and ethnicities. It does not mean you
understand everything about every ethnic group. But it does mean that
you have a love for and commitment to people to the point where you
will not likely permit ethnic, racial or cultural barriers to undermine
your relationships. It means you are able to live out the gifts of biculturalism in numerous ethnic and cultural settings.

A friend of mine named David Flores pastors a predominantly White
church in Westchester, a suburb of New York City. I have seen him interact very well with all sorts of people, including his White congrega-
tion; Latinos I introduced to him for the first time; people like my sister-
in-law Delba, who is mentally challenged; young teenagers like my eld-
est son, Daniel; strangers on the basketball court; and a group of Asian
Americans on a New York City campus.

Pastor David has and will continue to have a growing ministry because of his abilities to interact and connect with so many different kinds
of people. As bicultural Latinos we should aim to become as multicultural as we can as a way to serve Christ and others lovingly and effectively.

QUESTIONS FOR DISCUSSION AND REFLECTION

1. What are some areas in which you have seen your biculturalism, or
someone else's, as a strength?

2. How has God used you as a cultural interpreter?

3. How has God used your biculturalism to cross ethnic, racial or cultural boundaries?

4. As doors open up for you in the future, how will you determine which doors you will walk through?

5. Who is someone you admire who is multicultural? What have they been able to accomplish? What qualities of theirs would you like to emulate?

9

❊

HELPING OTHERS GROW IN THEIR ETHNIC IDENTITY

*I'm so glad my pastor told me about this weekend. I can't
believe it: I almost didn't come. I had no idea my attitude was
so messed up about being Colombian. I thought it didn't matter
anymore 'cause now I'm an American. I left my whole heritage
behind. I mean I don't even speak Spanish that much
anymore. Everybody here has helped me feel good about myself
and who I am. Now I'm really open to God to teach
me more about who I am.*

<small>STUDENT TESTIMONY AT THE END OF A LATINO FELLOWSHIP
(LAFE) CONFERENCE</small>

Finding wholeness in your ethnic identity does not have to end with
yourself. As followers of Christ we are called to share with others
what we have learned in our journey with God. This certainly includes sharing the insights we have gained regarding the value of
our ethnic identity. Developing a strong identity places us in a good

position to invest in the growth and maturity of others. It would have taken me much longer to gain wisdom had it not been for colleagues, friends and family who opened up their own ethnic journeys to me.

In this chapter I will give practical ideas on how to help others develop a healthy ethnic identity. I will draw on my experience and the experience of others who have invested in me.

FACILITATING OPPORTUNITIES FOR OTHERS

One of my greatest loves in the world is leading home groups where people build relationships and study Scripture in a nonthreatening setting. As the facilitator I get a thrill at gently leading participants into experiences that stretch them. I have discovered that even friendships do not just naturally happen. As an effective leader I must manage small group times in a way that draws people to love and value one another. In the same way, growth in our commitments to racial reconciliation, justice and ethnic identity development does not just happen. These are the issues we have become proficient as Christians at avoiding at all cost. Somehow, somewhere, someone must have the vision, the tenacity and the tools to lead others to them.

I have used a variety of group exercises designed to help participants explore their identity with others in a nonthreatening manner. The Latino Heritage Exercise, for example, gently leads people through a series of questions regarding family history, tradition, values, identity and race. When doing this exercise in groups, several ground rules are essential:

1. Each person must be given a sufficient amount of time to answer

all of the questions in the section you have chosen to work on together.

2. Do not attempt to have each person answer all the questions during one meeting. These work best when they are spread over three or four meetings, such as in a weekend retreat or a series of weekly meetings.

3. Participants may gently interrupt the person who is telling his or her story to ask clarifying questions directly related to the question being addressed. However, they should avoid making observations or responding prematurely.

4. Participants should openly show appreciation to all participants after they have told their stories. The leader, with the help of the group, can decide how best to do this.

5. A debriefing time after everyone has told their story should be led by the facilitator:

   a. How was this exercise helpful in getting to know each other from an ethnic perspective?

   b. What did you learn about each other that you didn't know before?

   c. Why is it helpful to understand who we are ethnically for our relationship with God and each other?

   d. What are some other things you feel you still need to explore in your ethnic journey and in your relationships with people of other racial or ethnic groups?

   e. Spend some time thanking God for each other's family, culture and relationships.

MY LATINO HERITAGE EXERCISE[1]

Name_____

Date_____

Part One: Mi Familia

Insert a photo of your family.

---

[1]This exercise was first developed by Gary Davis and Tom Hoppler in 1975 for an InterVarsity missions program entitled Student Training in Mission (STIM). It was modified over the years by Sam Barkat, former vice president of Multiethnic Ministry for InterVarsity, Neil Rendall and Orlando Crespo.

A. List your family members and their ages. Feel free to include some extended family members.

B. What do you admire about your parent(s)?

C. What food or smell reminds you of your home when you were young?

D. List two memorable family traditions.

E. List the most treasured gift you received from your parents.

F. Are there any ethnic components to the way your family expresses emotion?

G. List three characteristics or values learned from your family or Latino culture that you admire enough to make your own.

H. Origin: Draw your ancestors' trek to this country.

I. My Community

Insert a photo of your childhood home or community.

Part Two: Myself

Insert a photo of yourself under ten years of age.

A. List some of your personal traits, tastes and interests.

B. How do you describe yourself to others? Think of human groupings you consider yourself a part of—heritage, gender, class, generation, geographic origin. For example: Latino male, middle class, New York City, third generation.

C. If someone were to ask you about your identity, what would be your usual response? Does this response ever change? If yes, when and how? How is this identity important and meaningful to you?

D. What aspects of your Latino culture have helped you draw closer to God or seem biblically based? What aspects of your Latino culture have hindered you in your relationship with God and seem unbiblical?

Biblical and Helpful   *Unbiblical and Hindering*

E. What experiences have helped you to identify as a Latino?

F. What hurtful experiences have turned you away from identifying as a Latino?

G. Are there some Latino internal values and beliefs that have helped shape who you are? If so, please list these.

H. What are the ways God is encouraging you to grow in your Latino identity? What do you think are your next steps?

Part Three: Myself in Relationship to Others

A. What stereotypes of other Latinos did your family have?

B. What people groups did you and your family grow up fearing or distrusting?

C. What level of awareness of other cultures, including other Latino cultures, did you have growing up? How has your awareness changed since then? What one or two events have influenced your thinking?

D. What racial feelings or ideas helped shape you when you were growing up? How do you feel about these?

E. Describe a racial situation that impacted your life personally.

F. Reflect on an experience when you were in the minority. In the majority. What was it like for you?

G. Is race something Christians should address as an issue, or should Christians attempt to be "colorblind"?

CREATING A SAFE ENVIRONMENT

If we are to help others grow in their identity with intentional exercises like these, it is crucial for us to create a safe environment where no one is made to feel judged or inferior to anyone else. I have heard horror stories from Latino college students who decided to explore their cultural roots by joining a Latino club on campus. To their disappointment, they discovered that only students who already had a strong sense of ethnic self were welcomed. The group leaders had no patience for those who were still exploring their cultural and ethnic identity.

Such an environment is not conducive for growth but in fact shuts the door for those who are genuinely seeking to know themselves better. "If this attitude is a sign of what being Latino is all about, I'd rather forget the whole thing. I don't need them," one angry student said to me as he recalled his frustration at the time. Precious years had been lost in this student's ethnic journey.

Over the years I have led events across the country where Latinos reported having to deal with an air of cultural superiority from other Latinos. To offset this I have tried to make our events and conferences places of refuge for those who have experienced cultural confusion, fatigue and frustration. Participants are free to consider their ethnicity at their own pace and are encouraged to be open about their disappointments, thoughts and questions. We have been careful not to compare ourselves to one another in regards to our Spanish language proficiency, how in tune we are to Latino pop culture or how much we know about our history. My intention has been to help participants remain open to God and one another as they explore how God has shaped them. This has created a sense of freedom, openness and an appreciation without the pressure of having to prove one's ethnic allegiance or maturity.

NUESTRA FAMILIA: THE KEY TO UNDERSTANDING OURSELVES

Along with creating safety to explore issues of ethnicity, those of us in a position to guide others in their ethnic journeys must also help them realize that much of their growth will come from understanding and connecting to their family. Some of my Latino friends and colleagues distanced themselves from their family, unaware of the impact this would have on their long-term identity development. To face their family meant they would have to face the part of themselves they were most uncomfortable with.

Such was the case with a friend of mine named Daniel. In his college days he did everything within his power to stay far away from his family. He did not want to deal with his Dominican father, because deep down he knew he would have to face the good and the bad of his culture and identity. Only after moving out of New York City did he realize the importance of family in coming to terms with his Latino experience.

Several years ago, after an honest and painful conversation we had about family and identity, he decided to accept a pastoral position in the Washington Heights section of Manhattan, where his family lives, as a way to honestly explore his identity as a Dominican man. This has been a valuable and important part of his journey toward self-understanding, especially as he has had to confront issues of *machismo*. It has not been an easy journey, but it has been fruitful, as he has opened his heart to his family and reconciled with his father.

As mentors we do well to point people back to their families as a key step in bringing wholeness and clarity in their journey despite the inner turmoil they may experience.

STEPPING OUT IN LEADERSHIP

Placing Latinos in situations where they must lead other Latinos motivates them to seriously engage in questions about their own ethnicity. As they commit themselves to invest in another person's life, they are forced to wrestle with their own growth and maturity with a greater sense of dedication and purpose. Alcoholics Anonymous was founded on this bedrock idea: if you want to keep yourself from drinking, the best strategy is to help others stay sober. As you motivate and inspire them, you are motivating and inspiring yourself.

Several years ago a colleague of mine brought together key college students to help plan a Latino heritage event. Many of them came not knowing what to expect and lacking conviction for the need to even hold such an event. They came hesitant to enter in. As they met to plan, however, they began to tell their stories and share their struggles. They saw how much they had in common and how refreshing it was to be together. Slowly, as the weekend progressed and their ideas took shape, their level of understanding and commitment grew. They began to see the value of a heritage event as an investment in the lives of others struggling to know themselves. They were inspired to understand their own Latino heritage in order to invest in others.

The event was successful and has become a yearly gathering for Latinos searching to understand their identity. In fact, several of those who participated as leaders went on to become mentors and leaders in their Latino communities.

If we are truly committed to serving Christ and loving others, it is imperative that we invest in others who are struggling to understand themselves ethnically. Those of us who are farther along the road must be willing to turn back and lead others on some of the trails we have taken. It will mean intentionality and honest reflection on what has made a difference for us and how we can impart that to others.

Understanding our ethnic identity is not a science but an art that brings together the Spirit of God and the commitment of others who care. As we cooperate with the Spirit and open our hearts to understand all that God has made us, finding wholeness in our ethnic identity is not only possible but an incredibly enriching endeavor.

QUESTIONS FOR REFLECTION AND DISCUSSION

1. When and where have you been able to explore your identity in a "safe environment"?

2. How have you created safe environments for others to explore their ethnic identity?

3. How can your family help you understand your Latino experience better? What are some of your concerns about inviting them to help you in this area?

4. What are some leadership opportunities you can take advantage of to bless other Latinos? What are some of your concerns or hesitations?

10

A VISION FOR BEING LATINO IN CHRIST

"For I know the plans I have for you," declares the LORD,
"plans to prosper you and not to harm you, plans to give you
hope and a future. Then you will call upon me and come
and pray to me, and I will listen to you. You will seek me and
find me when you seek me with all your heart. I will be
found by you," declares the LORD, "and will bring you back
from captivity."

JEREMIAH 29:11-14

Being a Latino in Christ has led me to reflect on God's redemptive nature, how he brings blessing out of the "foolish things of this world." Our God takes pleasure in doing great things through that which appears weak in the eyes of human beings. "But God chose the foolish things of the world to shame the wise; God chose the weak things of the world to shame the strong. He chose the lowly things of this world and the despised things—and the things that are not—to nullify the things that are, so that no one may boast before him. . . . 'Let him who boasts boast in the Lord'" (1 Corinthians 1:27-29, 31). So much of what we do as American Latinos feels weak. Yet our weakness as misfits is our greatest source of strength, because it means that God, who loves to humble the exalted and exalt the humble, is for us and with us. Because of God's power and presence in us, we have the potential to bring together two worlds, through language or culture or any other way that brings out the best of both worlds and not the anticipated worst.

But only when we accept the embrace and affirmation of our Creator through Christ is this possible. Only when we know that God had a purpose when he made Latinos can we find lasting hope and meaning in our identity. We can no longer allow the majority culture and previous generations of Latinos to tell us who we are, because what comes back is always the same: "You are less than . . ." Only God sees us for who we are, a new creation, a third culture that can move forward to bring life and hope to new generations of Latinos who are lost in a labyrinth of confusion and complexity.

Latinos are beginning to live comfortably with these two worlds within. God is building in us this unity of identities, and one day they will be fused together. In addressing the work of reconciliation between Gentiles and Jews, Paul eloquently describes a new oneness in the Spirit that makes us one in Christ.

> For he himself is our peace, who has made the two one and has destroyed the barrier, the dividing wall of hostility, by abolishing in his flesh the law with its commandments and regulations. His purpose was to create in himself one new man out of the two, thus making peace, and in this one body to reconcile both of them to God through the cross, by which he put to death their hostility. He came and preached peace to you who were far away and peace to

those who were near. For through him we both have access to the Father by one Spirit. (Ephesians 2:14-18)

This passage is often used to address ethnic and racial tensions among Christians, to motivate us toward our true state of oneness through the person and work of Jesus Christ. It is this oneness that Latinos desperately long for *within ourselves*. As we allow the truth of God's power to bring unity within our own being and with others, American Latinos will be free to accomplish God's purposes in the world.

As we live out our dual identity, we can either become immobilized by the challenges or embrace the remarkable opportunities for ministry that open up for us as bridge people. What will it mean for us to live out the truth that God has plans for us to help in the advancement of the gospel in this country and beyond?

It was to the surviving elders of Jews taken into exile in Babylon, struggling with being Jewish in a foreign culture, that Jeremiah sent the words that appear at the beginning of this chapter—and more: "'When seventy years are completed for Babylon, I will come to you and fulfill my gracious promise to bring you back to this place. For I know the plans I have for you,' declares the LORD" (Jeremiah 29:10-11).

Even in the midst of exile God had plans for his people. And in the midst of our difficulties, such as living in a foreign land with no real land to return to because we are strangers even in the places of our birth and ancestry, God tells us that he has plans for our good, for our success in this foreign yet familiar land that is our home. A land that belonged not to White Americans but to Native Americans, the *mestizo* of Spanish and Indian confluence, and those whose lineage can be tracked beyond the arrival of Western European colonizers. Our new identity as Latinos and as God's people requires us to live with a strong and clear vision of who we are as American Latinos and the plans God has prepared us to accomplish.

These plans include stepping up to all kinds of leadership in this country. In decades to come it is very likely that Latinos will become the majority population in the United States. It is sobering to recall, given this reality, that there are still relatively very few Latinos in politics, midsized and large businesses, and other important positions of leadership and influence in this country. Our educational system is in such shambles that we are not training future generations academically to take up the mantle of leadership and contribute to making this country a better nation. In *Mañana: Christian Theology from a Hispanic Perspective*, Justo González warns us that we are in danger of becoming a sort of apartheid state as far as leadership is concerned. We are in peril of becoming a majority Latino country that is led primarily by Whites who, while no longer the majority, would still hold most of the power and authority.

My concern is not that Latinos hold all the power. The Bible is clear that all power belongs to God. We are merely stewards, and human handling of power must happen under the guidance and tutelage of a watchful God and with our humble awareness that our hearts are deceitful. However, it is a question of justice and fairness. Because our hearts are deceptive, the best safeguard for us is to share all of God's resources and for all peoples in a nation to be represented adequately.

This will mean more Latinos—and Latino advocates—need to develop leadership skills and be willing to step up, take a risk and lead. My hope in writing this book is that we deal directly with issues of ethnic identity to bring healing to our souls and move ahead to serve Christ with fewer limitations, be they physical, economic or psychological. Ethnic identity is not an end in itself but a means to getting all the pieces of our lives in order so that we are in a better place to love ourselves, our neighbors and our God.

My hope for your life is that you will attain heights you never thought possible and that you would live in peace within yourself. Jesus said, "Peace I leave with you; my peace I give you. I do not give to you as the world gives. Do not let your hearts be troubled and do not be afraid" (John 14:27). As we allow God to help us overcome the troubles that proceed from issues of identity, we will be liberated to love fully and receive love from others without reservation.

Let us be careful not to make ethnic identity an idol. We must invite God into our ethnic journey so that through his Spirit our eyes and hearts would be open to its proper place in our life and in our mission. González cautions us wisely:

> Let us not so idolize our culture that we oppress another Hispanic who does not speak as we do, or even one who never learned how to speak Spanish, because the pressures of society were too great. What will be most important in our attempts to rediscover the original liberating gospel will not be our participation in Spanish culture but our participation, jointly with the early church, with Jesus and the apostles, and with Afro-Americans and Asian Americans, in the condition of a dispossessed minority whom God is calling to new life. . . . While the cultural focus of Hispanic identity is exclusively our own, the social focus is something we share with many others in this country.[1]

I end with this prayer of blessing for you and for us:

---

[1]Justo González, *Mañana: Christian Theology from a Hispanic Perspective* (Nashville: Abingdon, 1990), p. 38.

Heavenly Father, help us to find our identity in you. Help us to understand all that you have made us so that we might live to glorify you and make you known to others. I pray you will bless all people, but because you are a God of the dispossessed and a God who cares for the poor, I pray for the Latino community in this country. Heal our inner turmoil once and for all. Free us like birds to sail across the sky in freedom to be who you have made us. Lead us to the purposes for which you have created us, and teach us to live in complete and utter dependence on your leadership and your love for all people, through Jesus Christ, our Savior and our God. Amen.

QUESTIONS FOR REFLECTION AND DISCUSSION

1. As we seek to understand our ethnic identity, how is this connected to our awareness of ourselves in relationship to God?

2. Why is it important to embrace God's love and purpose for us as we develop in our ethnic identity?

3. Imagine you could sit down with God and influence his plans regarding American Latinos. What would be your recommendations? Don't be afraid to dream big.

4. Write your own prayer of blessing for Latinos in America.

APPENDIX 1

LATINO RACISM AND CONFLICT IN THE UNITED STATES

1740-1830: Acts of Violence in the United States and the Southwest
During these ninety years Whites and Mexicans clashed with one another many times. Because of their subordinate status, Mexicans were often the ones who suffered as the victims of violence such as discrimination, murders, thefts, land invasion and other gross miscarriages of justice.

1846: The Mexican War
Concerned that the annexation of Texas was an act of aggression, the Mexican government broke off diplomatic relations with the United States in 1845. President Polk sent a diplomat to Mexico to buy California and New Mexico for $25 million. When the Mexican government refused the offer, the United States declared war on Mexico.[1]

1848: The Treaty of Guadalupe Hidalgo
The Treaty of Guadalupe Hidalgo signed on February 2, 1848, officially

---

[1]Novas Himilce, *Everything You Need to Know About Latino History* (New York: Penguin, 1994), p. 77.

ended the Mexican War by handing over California, Utah, Nevada, and parts of Colorado, Wyoming, New Mexico and Arizona to the United States. After the treaty was signed, most of the important paragraphs that did not suit U.S. senators were deleted without the knowledge of the Mexicans. Many Mexicans who decided to become American citizens lost their land and their homes to encroaching homesteaders because they did not have written proof of ownership needed in the U.S. courts.

1857: The Cart War, South Texas
Seventy-five Mexicans were attacked and murdered by White cartmen.

1859-1860: Cheno Cortina Raids, Brownsville, Texas
Juan Nepomuceno Cortino and sixty of his men fought White lawmen as racial incidents increased. Fifteen Americans and eight Mexicans died in the raids.

1863: Only Woman Hanged in Texas History
After being found guilty of murdering a horse trader named John Savage, Chipita Rodriguez was hanged despite weak evidence and the jury's recommendation for mercy. She was the only woman ever hanged in Texas history.[2]

1870s: Trouble on the Border
Indian raids and bandit activity reached crisis level in the United States and Mexico. Hundreds were killed, property was destroyed, and national sovereignty was repeatedly violated.

---

[2]Nicolas Kanellos, *Hispanic Firsts* (Detroit: Visible Ink, 1997), p. 112.

1871: Mesilla Riots, Mesilla, New Mexico

Nine Spanish-speaking men were killed and forty to fifty others wounded, most of them supporters of politician Colonel J. Francisco Chavez.

1873: Lincoln County War, New Mexico

Thirteen Mexicans were killed, trapped in the middle of a range war between rival White cattlemen. Many Whites were also killed.

1877: The Salt War, El Paso, Texas

Mexicans from San Elizario rebelled against White entrepreneurs who had taken over community salt deposits. Texas Rangers were unsuccessful in reestablishing peace. Whites and Mexicans died in the violent clashes and executions that followed.

1880s: Panhandle, Texas

Retaliating for the murder of a White sheepman, Texas cowboys rampaged in Tascosa, killing several innocent Mexicans and lynching others suspected of complicity in the murder. Gunman and folk hero Sostenes l'Archeveque, of French-Mexican descent, was identified as the killer and was executed in a trap.

1898: U.S. Invasion of Puerto Rico

U.S. troops invaded Puerto Rico just five months after the island had fought for and acquired independence from Spain. Washington, D.C., politicians regarded the Puerto Rican people as an inferior race. In 1900 Senator Henry M. Teller of Colorado frankly admitted, "I don't like the Puerto Rican. . . . Such a race is unworthy of citizenship." Senator Bate of Tennessee described the people of the Philippines and Puerto Rico as "savages addicted to head-hunting and cannibalism."[3]

1900: El Carmen, Texas

While Gregorio Cortez was in his home with his brother and the rest of his family, a sheriff entered and asked him about a missing mare. A misunderstanding arose and the sheriff shot Cortez's brother, killing him. Cortez shot the sheriff, thus becoming an outlaw. Eventually he was caught, put on trial and found not guilty. He was put on trial again for having stolen a mare, was found guilty and sentenced to ninety-nine years and a day. A year later Abraham Lincoln's daughter asked the Texas governor for clemency. Cortez was set free but soon after was poisoned and killed by his enemies.

1915-1916: Plan of San Diego Raids, Texas-Tamaulipas Border

Raids associated with the Plan of San Diego, a widespread plot to fight against civil rights abuses by overthrowing U.S. rule of former Mexican territories, kept the Texas Lower Rio Grande Valley in continuous turmoil. Raiders included Mexican revolutionaries, Mexican American guerrillas and bandits of various backgrounds. U.S. troops, Texas Rangers, local lawmen and vigilantes retaliated against the attackers, sometimes crossing into Mexico to avenge losses. Hundreds died in the raids.

1917: Passage of the Jones Act

Puerto Ricans became American citizens after the passage of the Jones Act by the U.S. Congress. The island remained a colony with very little

---

[3]Jane Norling, *Puerto Rico: Flame of Resistance* (San Francisco: People's Press, 1977), p. 35.

self-determination. However, they were denied full representation in American politics as they were not entitled to elected representation in Congress.[4]

1930s: San Francisco, California

Lewis Terman at Stanford University announced that Latino children were incapable of competing intellectually with White children. Terman's statement was used to justify racist policies in the first half of the twentieth century. "Latinos were expected to do poorly in school and then to drop out. Those who stayed on past elementary school were consigned to trade schools. Children who had difficulty with English were treated like the feeble-minded in schools from Texas to California."[5]

1937: Ponce Massacre, Ponce, Puerto Rico

Twenty people were killed and 150 were wounded by policemen using machine guns and rifles during a protest march in support of Nationalist leader Pedro Albizo Campos. See chapter one.

1943: Zoot Suit Riots, Los Angeles, California

A brawl began, instigated by a group of U.S. Marines and sailors from Oakland. As they beat up Blacks and Mexican Americans, the police watched and eventually responded by arresting the victimized Mexican American youth and accusing them of disturbing the peace. The clashes worsened until rioting broke out on June 7. Chicanos and other racial and ethnic groups were targets in restaurants and other public areas. About six hundred Chicanos were arrested. Newspapers praised the po-

---

[4]Kanellos, *Hispanic Firsts*, p.117.
[5]Earl Shorris, *Latinos: A Biography of the People* (New York: W. W. Norton & Company, 1992), p. 156.

lice, who claimed the arrests were necessary to prevent further violence. The incident sparked White racist attacks on Mexican Americans in Beaumont, Texas; Chicago; San Diego; Detroit; Evansville, Indiana; Philadelphia; and New York City.

1953-1956: Operation Wetback
After World War II ended and soldiers returned home seeking employment, two million Mexicans who had provided cheap labor in the United States were sent back to Mexico in what became known as Operation Wetback.

1960s: Cesar Chavez's Activism, California
To fight numerous injustices in the treatment and working conditions of Chicano and Filipino farmworkers, Cesar Chavez organized workers into the United Farm Workers Union (UFW). A widespread boycott of grapes ended when California grape growers signed a contract with the union. Chavez and the UFW transformed the boycott into a movement of social justice for farm workers, which later led to widespread changes in wages, working conditions, the safe use of pesticides and the right to strike and form unions.[6]

1980: Cuban Marielitas Arrive in Florida
Tens of thousands of Cubans were permitted by Castro to leave Cuba. When they arrived at Mariel Harbor in Florida, the Cubans, who were poor, uneducated and racially mixed, were housed in tent cities and football stadiums. They became frustrated over long delays in being able to leave the camps. Many were forced to remain in the camps for years before being released.

---

[6]Kanellos, *Hispanic Firsts,* p.147.

1987: Negative Stereotypes in Education

Lloyd Dunn developed a psychological test used to determine how children should be educated. He wrote these words in a monograph titled *Bilingual Children on the US Mainland: Review of Research on Their Cognitive, Linguistic and Scholastic Development:* "While many people are willing to blame the low scores of Puerto Ricans and Mexican Americans on their poor environmental conditions, few are prepared to face the probability that inherited genetic material is a contributing factor."[7]

1988: Midland, Texas

Over three hundred Latino FBI agents, claiming a longstanding pattern of discrimination by the FBI, took the bureau to court. Judge Lucius B. Denton found the agents' grievances justified, ruled in their favor and ordered the bureau to review promotions for Latinos.

1996: Washington, D.C.

As a response to injustices in education, the minimum wage, immigration and affirmative action, the first national Hispanic March for Justice took place in Washington, D.C., on October 12, 1996.

---

[7]Shorris, *Latinos*, p. 156.

APPENDIX 2

A Few Common Spanglish Words and Phrases

Dame un break, please. Give me a break, please.

Cógelo con take it easy. Take it slow and easy.*

Can you record my novela? Can you record my Spanish soap opera?*

Have you seen my chancletas? Have you seen my slippers?

Refrita. This has nothing to do with refried beans (frijoles). It's a term for being overworked (e.g., "My job has me so refrita, I need some rest").*

Un tíquet. Parking or speeding ticket (e.g., "He pulled me over to give me un tíquet").*

Juan guey. A directional phrase: one-way street.*

How chuposo. The perfect phrase to convey disgust or distaste (e.g., "I have an early meeting on Monday. How chuposo!").*

Estuckiado. Stuck or pinned down.

El esteeng. Heat from a steam radiator.

Rufo. Roof.

*Taken from *Latina Magazine*, May 2003 edition.

APPENDIX 3

LATINO BOOKS, FILMS AND WEBSITES

The following list was compiled by the author and Daniela Reynoso. Daniela is an InterVarsity Campus staffworker in San Francisco.

MOVIES AND DOCUMENTARIES

And the Earth Did Not Swallow Him (1994)
Directed by Severo Perez. "The year is 1952. A Mexican American family is struggling to survive, working as migrant laborers in fields from Texas to Minnesota. The younger son, Marcos, is a sensitive 12-year-old who is forced to confront the ineluctable facts of his life-grinding poverty, back-breaking work, racism, hopelessness. He manages to pull himself out of his miserable life, eventually becoming a professor and author of a landmark work of Chicano literature, *And the Earth Did Not Swallow Him*." (Gary Kamiya, San Francisco Examiner, Sept. 22, 1995). 99 min.

American Family (2001)
Produced by Gregory Nava, this PBS series takes a complex look at Chicano families and sociocultural, sociopolitical and socioeconomic realities affecting the family, such as poverty, gang activity, adoption and community violence. It restores dignity to the Chicano community by developing positive and complex characters.

Birthwrite: Growing Up Hispanic (1988)

Documentary by the Cinema Guild. Profiles Latino writers and how their works reflect growing up in the United States. 57 min.

El Norte (1983)

Directed by Gregory Nava. Beginning in the remote mountain jungles of Guatemala, awash with the lushness of nature and the rainbow colors of the Mayans, this highly acclaimed drama about a brother and sister seeking a better life centers on two young Indians. When their father is killed by government soldiers and their mother taken away, they set out for the "promised land" to the north—El Norte. When they finally reach Los Angeles, however, their trials are not over for they are "illegals" submerged in an alien culture. 141 min.

Frida (2002)

Directed by Julie Taymor. Salma Hayek plays the Mexican surrealist painter Frida Kahlo, whose tempestuous life with her unfaithful husband, muralist Diego Rivera (Alfred Molina), drives the story of Frida. Director Julie Taymor pulls out a wealth of gorgeous visuals to capture everything from the horrific bus accident that damaged Kahlo's spine to her and Rivera's trip to New York City, where Rivera's political leanings ruptured a commission from the Rockefeller family. Taymor's dynamic energy and Hayek's forceful performance give Frida genuine emotional impact. 123 min.

How We Feel: Hispanic Students Speak Out (1990)

Documentary by Landmark Educational Media. College-bound students suggest ways to improve American education for Latinos. 21 min.

La Ciudad (The City) (1998)

Directed by David Riker. Filmed through intensive collaboration with the New York Latino immigrant community over a five-year period, *La Ciudad* tells four stories about recently arrived illegal immigrants from Mexico and Latin America to New York City, weaving a rich narrative tapestry of present-day immigrant life. The film's four stories center on a group of day laborers scavenging for bricks, two teenagers from the same hometown who meet in the projects and fall in love, a homeless father who tries to enroll his daughter in school, and a garment worker who seeks justice in the sweatshops. 88 min.

Mi Puerto Rico (1996)

Directed by Raquel Ortiz. Documentary by the National Latino Communications Center Educational Media. Relates the personal experience of Ortiz, who grows up in New York and then goes back to Puerto Rico to find her roots. 90 min.

Milagro Beanfield Wars (1988)

Produced and directed by Robert Redford. Starring Ruben Blades, Richard Bradford, Sonia Braga, Julie Carmen, James Gammon, Melanie Griffith, John Heard, Carlos Riquelme, Daniel Stern, Christopher Walken and Chick Vennera. In this fable set in a magical New Mexican village, everyday people are caught up in extraordinary circumstances. Based on the novel by John Treadwell Nichols. 118 min.

My Family/Mi Familia (1995)

Directed by Gregory Nava. Starring Edward James Olmos, Esai Morales and Jimmy Smitts, this movie follows a family from their migration to Los Angeles from Mexico, to the birth of their grandchildren. Along the way, the parents fall in love, the mother is unlawfully deported to Mexico, a son serves prison time and another son attends a prestigious law school. This movie is told from the perspective of the writer in the family. 126 min.

Real Women Have Curves (2002)

This is a coming of age story about a Chicana growing up in East L.A. who recently graduated from high school in Beverly Hills. Whether the topic is work, dating or family, she is constantly making decisions between her family's cultural expectations and her desire to live life with freedom and independence. 85 min.

Romero (1989)

Starring Raul Julia, this is a provocative movie about the life of Oscar Romero, the archbishop of El Salvador during the years of 1977-1980. Romero's life becomes compromised because his faith requires him to take a bold stand against the government and the wealthy land-owning elite. 105 min.

Stand and Deliver (1987)

Directed by Ramon Menendez. Jaime Escalante, a math teacher at East Los Angeles's Garfield High School, refuses to write off his kids as losers. He cajoles, pushes, wheedles, needles, threatens and inspires eighteen kids to become math whizzes. Then they take the National Advanced Placement Calculus exam with surprising results. 103 min.

Zoot Suit (1981)

Directed by Luis Valdez. A group of Mexican Americans are sent to San Quentin unjustly for the death of a man at Sleepy Lagoon. Based on the actual case and Zoot Suit Riots of 1940s Los Angeles. 108 min.

BOOKS

Fiction

Cisneros, Sandra. *Woman Hollering Creek, and Other Stories*. New York: Random House, 1991.

> The characters in this collection of vignettes share accounts of living in both the United States and Mexico. These stories skillfully and comically shed light on living life as a bicultural person in society.

Garcia, Cristina. *Dreaming in Cuban*. New York: Ballantine, 1992.

> This novel follows three generations of Cuban women and their family's journey into life in the U.S.

Rodriguez, Richard. *An Argument with My Mexican Father*. New York: Penguin, 1993.

> A brilliant essay that eloquently deals with the complexity of redefining how we think about ethnicity, education and religion in America.

Santiago, Esmeralda. *When I Was Puerto Rican*. New York: 1st Vintage Books, 1994.

> This is a coming of age memoir of Esmeralda Santiago told with love and tenderness as she moves to New York City from Puerto Rico and overcomes difficulties.

Viramontes, Helena Maria. *Under the Feet of Jesus*. New York: Plume, 1995.

> This coming of age story of a Chicana among migrant workers in California offers wonderful spiritual metaphors to convey the author's experience.

Historical Background and Accuracy

Higham, John. *Strangers in the Land: Patterns of American Nativism, 1860-1925*. New Brunswick, N.J.: Rutgers University Press, 1994.

> Highman describes nativism as "every type and level of antipathy to-

wards aliens, their institutions, and their ideas" (p. 3). This author critically analyzes some of the historical roots of anti-immigrant sentiment in the United States by tracing significant events such as White intrusion of Indigenous America to Americanization programs and immigration policy.

Gonzalez, Juan. *Harvest of Empire: A History of Latinos in America*. New York: Penguin, 2000.

This sweeping history of Latinos in America also offers a look at family portraits of real-life immigrant Latino pioneers and their reasons for leaving their homeland.

Novas, Hilmilce. *Everything You Need to Know About Latino History*. New York: Plume, 1998.

This readable reference work focuses on the history, culture, politics, sports, food and fashion of Latinos. It seeks to answer many questions people ask about the Latino experience in America.

Sánchez, George J. *Becoming Mexican American: Ethnicity, Culture, and Identity in Chicano Los Angeles, 1900-1945*. New York: Oxford University Press, 1993.

Sánchez gives voice to Chicano life in L.A. through events, policy, employment patterns, and other sociopolitical and sociocultural realities. This book is illuminating and provocative.

Vargas, Zaragosa, ed. *Major Problems in Mexican American History*. Boston: Houghton Mifflin, 1999.

This book is one topic in the series Major Problems in American History. History is often written with a cultural bias toward those in power. This series compiles original documents and essays surrounding highlighted events and offers resources for further reading to allow our own critical examination of these events. Vargas studies events and themes in Mexican American history from precolonial to contemporary America.

Weber, David J., ed. *Foreigners in Their Native Land: Historical Roots of the Mexican Americans.* Albuquerque: University of New Mexico Press, 1973.

> Weber traces U.S. invasion of Mexican Territory and the development of the Mexican American identity through firsthand accounts of society in the Southwest during nineteenth-century America. He lays a solid foundation to better understand contemporary Mexican American identity and realities.

Memoirs

Augenbraum, Harold, and Ilan Stavans. *Growing Up Latino: Memoirs and Stories.* Boston: Houghton Mifflin, 1993.

> This anthology of recent Latino fiction and nonfiction deals with such issues as religion, sex, love, language and family. It also shatters the idea there is one Latino experience in America.

Cofer, Judith Ortiz. *Silent Dancing: A Partial Remembrance of a Puerto Rican Childhood.* Houston: Arte Público Press, 1990.

> This novel is a memoir of one woman's childhood, growing up in both Puerto Rico and New York.

O'Hearn, Claudine Chiawei, ed. *Half + Half: Writers on Growing up Biracial + Bicultural.* New York: Pantheon, 1998.

> This collection features Latino writers Juila Alavarez and Ruben Martinez. The additional contributors also offer poignant insights.

Navarette, Ruben, Jr. *A Darker Shade of Crimson.* New York: Bantam, 1994.

> A young Mexican American chronicles his life from California's San Joaquin Valley to the halls of Harvard University in 1985. He is forced to confront issues of identity, ethnicity, race, family and education.

Villaseñor, Victor. *Rain of Gold.* New York: Laurel, 1991.

> This nonfiction book reads like a novel. Villaseñor first traces the par-

allel lives of his parents and then recounts the story of how they met. In the process, he describes his family's experiences of poverty, violence, racism and migration as they sought a better life for themselves as migrant farm workers.

Policy

Piatt, Bill. *Black and Brown in America: The Case for Cooperation.* New York: New York University Press, 1997.

This book discusses the history of African American and Hispanic relations in the United States and offers challenges to both groups on moving forward together. Chapters include "How Did We Get Here?" "Jobs: Competing for a Shrinking Pie?" "Language: Speaking to, and About, One Another" and "Voting: Coalition or Collision?"

Smith, Anna Deavere. *Twilight: Los Angeles, 1992.* New York: Anchor Books, 1994.

This play, based on collections of interviews of people affected by the civil unrest in Los Angeles in 1992, takes an incredible look into race relations in L.A. Latinos, Anglos, African Americans, Koreans—all get a chance to speak.

Torre, Adela de la. *Moving from the Margins: A Chicana Voice on Public Policy.* Tucson: University of Arizona Press, 2002.

This is a great book for those who want to gain a better understanding of contemporary policy issues affecting the Latino community. Torre discusses health care, education, immigration and other hot-button issues.

Sociology

Anzaldua, Gloria. *Borderlands, La Frontera: The New Mestiza.* San Francisco: Aunt Lute Books, 1987.

Anzaldua discusses some of the historical and social realities of life on the U.S.-Mexican border and uses the borderlands to discuss psychological, sexual and spiritual borderlands. She offers a historical account of the creation of borders through events of colonization and also offers critique of sociocultural expectations of men and women.

Gil, Rosa Maria, and Carmen Inoa Vazquez. *The Maria Paradox: How Latinas can Merge Old World Traditions with New World Self-Esteem.* New York: G.P. Putnam's Sons, 1996.

These authors describe the cult of femininity in the Latino community, *marianismo*, and offer critique and analysis as to its effect on Latinas. They also offer advice to empower Latinas to lead life, whether at work or at home, with integrity and self-respect.

Morales, Ed. *Living in Spanglish.* New York: St. Martin's Press, 2002.

This book gives a fresh perspective that highlights the commonalities Latinos in America share with one another. He calls this commonality Spanglish: a feeling, an attitude and a language that captures the essence of the Latino experience in America.

Rodriguez, Clara E., and Virginia Sanchez Korrol. *Historical Perspectives on Puerto Rican Survival in the United States.* Princeton, N.J.: Markus Weiner, 1996.

This book is a collection of classic articles on important Puerto Rican themes such as the Young Lords, Latin music, Puerto Rican women, race within ethnicity and more.

Stavans, Ilan. *The Hispanic Condition: Reflections on Culture and Identity in America.* New York: HarperCollins, 1995.

Personal reflection has led Stavans to a larger and deeper understanding of Latinos in the United States. He does not give one profile of the Latino identity. Instead, he analyzes historical and sociocultural realities to communicate common themes affecting the Latino community.

This book also offers appendixes of historical chronology and of selected sources for further study.

Theology

Aquino, María Pilar, Daisy L. Machado, and Jeannette Rodríguez, eds. *A Reader in Latina Feminist Theology: Religion & Justice.* Austin, Tex.: University of Austin Press, 2002.

This is a great book of collected articles on Latina identity, cultural icons and double standards in our society. It discusses God's redemption of culture and identity.

Costas, Orlando E. *Christ Outside the Gate: Mission Beyond Christendom.* Maryknoll, N.Y.: Orbis, 1982.

A comprehensive analysis of the missiological issues facing the church including the need to contextualize the gospel.

Elizondo, Virgilio. *Galilean Journey: The Mexican-American Promise.* Maryknoll, N.Y.: Orbis, 2000.

Elizondo looks at the sociocultural reality of *mestizaje*—the mingling of ethnicity, race and culture—among Mexican Americans and uses this theme to illuminate the complexity of Jesus' identity as a marginalized Galilean. The person of Jesus can speak to life as a *mestizo*.

González, Justo L. *Mañana: Christian Theology from a Hispanic Perspective.* Nashville: Abingdon, 1990.

González discusses identity and contextualizes the gospel to the experiences of Latino people. He offers some great discourse and critique on the simplification and spiritualization of the gospel. The gospel is supposed to be relevant in tangible ways, and this author shows how such is true today.

González, Justo L. *Santa Biblia: The Bible Through Hispanic Eyes.* Nashville: Abingdon, 1996.

González offers paradigms to study the Bible from the perspective of the greater Latino community and to make the gospel relevant.

Maldonado, David, Jr., ed. *Protestantes/Protestants: Hispanic Christianity Within Mainline Traditions.* Nashville: Abingdon, 1999.

This multi-author book explores the historical dynamics that motivated Protestant missionaries and their denominational strategies.

Ortiz, Manuel. *The Hispanic Challenge: Opportunities Confronting the Church.* Downers Grove, Ill.: InterVarsity Press, 1993.

This pastor from Chicago discusses a few of the blessings and challenges in seeing the gospel go forth from the Latino in the inner city. He discusses the necessity of solidarity and reconciliation with other marginalized communities (specifically the African American community) and discusses the need for support and development of Latino leaders.

Rodriguez, Jose David, and Loida I. Martell-Otero, eds. *Teologia en Conjunto.* Louisville, Ky.: Westminster John Knox, 1997.

This is a collaborative work in which Latino Protestants in North America discuss theological topics such as God, Jesus Christ, the Holy Spirit, Scripture, the church, humanity, the doctrine of sin, spirituality and other challenges facing Latino theology.

Perez, Arturo, Consuelo Covarrubias and Edward Foley, eds. *Asi Es: Stories of Hispanic Spirituality.* Collegeville, Minn.: Liturgical Press, 1994.

This book is a collection of faith experiences of Latino Catholic believers—some nuns, some priests, some parishioners. Many of these accounts look at the love of God as manifested through family and migration.

Pope-Levison, Priscilla, and John R. Levison. *Jesus in Global Contexts.* Louisville, Ky.: Westminster John Knox, 1992.

This book is a great, easy to swallow introduction to liberation theology.

Sobrino, Jon. *Christology at the Crossroads: A Latin American Approach.*
Maryknoll, N.Y.: Orbis, 1978.
> Sobrino offers a much deeper look into liberation theology (specifically the nature of Jesus) by one of the greatest liberation theologians.

LATINO WEBSITES

www.amarillas.com
A Latino yellow pages with a directory of links to Latino places of interest on the web.

hispanicfund.org
Hispanic College Fund

hsfi.org
Hispanic Scholarship Fund Institute

hisp.com
Hispanic Magazine

latinolink.com
This site offers Latino-oriented chat forums, literature, music, entertainment, politics, business, travel and more.

latinoweb.com
This site explores Latino and Latin American culture, music, film and art.

lulac.org
League of United Latin American Citizens

maldef.org

The Mexican American Legal Defense and Education Fund (MALDEF)

This organization advocates the civil rights of Mexican Americans in the educational system.

nclr.org

National Council of La Raza

This organization researches and advocates for the civil rights of Latinos in significant policy areas affecting the Latino community, such as immigration, health care and education.

ufw.org

United Farm Workers

This organization struggles to give farm workers a voice for their basic human rights, such as a livable wage and adequate health care, in the workplace.